COMPLETE
CONDITIONING
FOR SOCCER

Greg Gatz

Human Kinetics

Library of Congress Cataloging-in-Publication Data

Gatz, Greg.
 Complete conditioning for soccer / Greg Gatz.
    p. cm.
 Includes index.
 ISBN-13: 978-0-7360-7713-2 (soft cover)
 ISBN-10: 0-7360-7713-8 (soft cover)
 1. Soccer--Training. 2. Soccer--Physiological aspects. I. Title.
 GV943.9.T7G38 2009
 796.334--dc22

                               2008052941

ISBN-10: 0-7360-7713-8
ISBN-13: 978-0-7360-7713-2

This publication is written and published to provide accurate and authoritative information relevant to the subject matter presented. It is published and sold with the understanding that the author and publisher are not engaged in rendering legal, medical, or other professional services by reason of their authorship or publication of this work. If medical or other expert assistance is required, the services of a competent professional person should be sought.

Acquisitions Editor: Tom Heine; **Developmental Editor:** Leigh Keylock; **Assistant Editor:** Laura Podeschi; **Copyeditor:** Patsy Fortney; **Proofreader:** Jim Burns; **Indexer:** Betty Frizzéll; **Permission Manager:** Martha Gullo; **Graphic Designer:** Fred Starbird; **Graphic Artist:** Francine Hamerski; **Cover Designer:** Keith Blomberg; **Photographer (cover):** Denis Doyle/Getty Images; photo icon on page v © Human Kinetics; **Technique Videographers:** Gregg Henness and Bill Yauch; **Photo Asset Manager:** Laura Fitch; **Video Production Coordinator:** Amy Rose; **Photo Production Manager:** Jason Allen; **Art Manager:** Kelly Hendren; **Associate Art Manager and Illustrator:** Alan L. Wilborn; **Printer:** United Graphics

Human Kinetics books are available at special discounts for bulk purchase. Special editions or book excerpts can also be created to specification. For details, contact the Special Sales Manager at Human Kinetics.

Printed in the United States of America   10 9 8 7 6 5 4 3 2 1

Human Kinetics
Web site: www.HumanKinetics.com

United States: Human Kinetics
P.O. Box 5076
Champaign, IL 61825-5076
800-747-4457
e-mail: humank@hkusa.com

Canada: Human Kinetics
475 Devonshire Road Unit 100
Windsor, ON N8Y 2L5
800-465-7301 (in Canada only)
e-mail: info@hkcanada.com

Europe: Human Kinetics
107 Bradford Road
Stanningley
Leeds LS28 6AT, United Kingdom
+44 (0) 113 255 5665
e-mail: hk@hkeurope.com

Australia: Human Kinetics
57A Price Avenue
Lower Mitcham, South Australia 5062
08 8372 0999
e-mail: info@hkaustralia.com

New Zealand: Human Kinetics
Division of Sports Distributors NZ Ltd.
P.O. Box 300 226 Albany
North Shore City
Auckland
0064 9 448 1207
e-mail: info@humankinetics.co.nz

COMPLETE CONDITIONING FOR SOCCER

Contents

DVD Contents

Speed

Agility

Peak Conditioning for the Game

Total Running Time .64 minutes

Preface

The game of soccer is dynamic and multifaceted. Performing successfully at a high level requires many skills including balance, agility, power, and speed. Whether you are carving up an opponent's defense with fast footwork and quickness or delivering a powerful knockout shot beyond the keeper's reach, you need these skills to raise your performance on the pitch. For this you need a strong foundation. Fortunately, these skills can be trained using a progressive, specific, and tailored program that can improve your performance. This book shows you how to use each of the training components to create a complete and efficient conditioning program.

The purpose of *Complete Conditioning for Soccer* is to lay out a plan to develop championship-level soccer performance using the training philosophy, methods, and drills (exercises) that are suited to soccer's demands. This book will challenge you by offering a progressive, long-term approach to improving athleticism for soccer. You will gain an understanding of the fitness components that apply to the game and learn how to develop a total training package that addresses each one.

Today, performance training for soccer has become quite sophisticated. The concept of playing yourself into shape has been replaced with specific drills and exercises that replicate game experiences and improve overall performance. More time is now dedicated to improving strength and fitness levels to gain performance advantages that top-level players did not have years ago. Using current information, this book will guide you through each training component so you can create a logical plan.

Chapter 1 describes the physical demands of soccer and the kinds of training needed to improve the various components required in the game. Chapter 2 introduces a method of evaluating individual starting strength and fitness levels to gain an understanding of fitness needs and deficiencies. It offers an easy step-by-step guide to various tests used to analyze total-body flexibility, strength, power, agility, quickness, and speed. This battery of tests will give quick feedback so you can develop training plans to meet your individual needs.

Chapter 3 describes a dynamic method for increasing flexibility and joint range of motion to improve agility, speed, and quickness. This chapter provides a variety of routines to incorporate into your training.

Balance training, discussed in chapter 4, can build a stable foundation to help control high-speed movements during matches. The series of exercises in this chapter will develop both static and dynamic balance. This foundational work will increase coordination and the execution of motor skills that you will notice on the field. Chapter 5 provides valuable information to increase hip and leg strength to develop the total-body power used when performing in the game. Special attention is given to the strength needs of the female athlete.

As you move through the basic foundational components (flexibility, strength, and balance), you will begin to see how this work supports the more dynamic components (power, agility, and speed), which will increase performance in soccer-specific movements. Power is discussed in chapter 6.

Speed and acceleration in the game of soccer can be the most critical area in your repertoire. It is an area that can make or break your ability to "make the play." Chapter 7 addresses speed components, teaching you how to analyze your running technique so you can increase your foot speed and develop top-end speed to improve on-field performance.

Agility training, comprised of footwork, change of direction, and reaction time, is presented in chapter 8. Specific drills aimed at improving stopping and reaccelerating mechanics are presented. Improving agility will help you change direction and gain a step on the opponent.

Chapter 9 discusses the energy demands of soccer and presents a plan to raise your level of fitness. These drills incorporate general conditioning along with position-specific training to elevate and sustain performance.

Chapter 10 addresses match readiness. Both single- and multiple-match scenarios are discussed, and sample warm-up, strength training, and conditioning sessions are reviewed. The chapter also includes a warm-up routine designed for substitutions coming off the bench, a post-halftime warm-up to restart the body after intermission, and a postmatch cool-down.

Chapter 11 is devoted to injury prevention and recovery, clarifying the proper protocol for minimizing the risk of injuries that can occur during the game. Part of this protocol involves regeneration techniques after stressful workouts that help bring your body back to a balanced state.

The final chapter of the book sequences all the training components into a comprehensive training plan that you can use throughout the year. The sequence takes into consideration both competitive and noncompetitive training periods. A special section includes exercises that can be performed on the field during the competitive season for efficiency.

The training DVD included with this book will help to enhance your knowledge of conditioning for soccer. This DVD defines the techniques of the most complex exercises, offering additional tips and recommendations; it offers visual demonstrations that you can refer to over and over. The exercises that appear on the DVD are listed on pages vi and vii, and they are also marked with this symbol in the text: ◉ **DVD**.

Throughout the book, where yards is used as a unit of measurement, the reader can insert meters and vice versa, given that the two are very similar in length.

Whether you are new to training or an experienced player, *Complete Conditioning for Soccer* has something for you. Knowing how to construct an individual conditioning program will give you the advantage of bringing your performance on the field to new heights and help you stay ahead of the competition. Building the basic components that comprise your athletic profile will set the cornerstone for advancing your soccer playmaking abilities. Let's start the process by identifying the demands the game of soccer poses. With a combination of consistency and determination, you will be well on your way to achieving your soccer ambitions!

Chapter 1

The Physical Demands of Soccer

Many people perceive athletic ability as natural, inherent talent. When witnessing the graceful, fluid movements of many talented athletes, you can understand why they are viewed as extraordinary. Soccer players are no exception. The game reveals nonstop athletic duels that require coordinated patterns of sprinting, jumping, feinting, kicking, and passing for 90 minutes. Although most talent is innate, the majority of soccer fitness components can be trained to elevate play to a higher level. The method you use to train these qualities will be a key ingredient in sharpening your overall skills on the field.

To develop an effective training program, you must first understand the demands of soccer. The fitness foundation for soccer consists of many components: flexibility, balance, strength, power, speed, agility, and endurance. The emphasis on each component can be adjusted to fit your individual goals and needs, but training all the components at least minimally will yield a synergistic effect to performance. One mistake many athletes make is to develop one component more than others, leading to imbalances. A good example of this is the player who incorporates a steady diet of distance running in training. Although soccer requires the aerobic energy system, and endurance will improve by training it, the ability to accelerate explosively will be dampened by training exclusively at slower tempos.

Let's take a closer look at the following fitness components to understand their relationship to soccer performance. Each section discusses both general training for building athleticism and specific training for developing soccer-specific fitness.

FLEXIBILITY

The game of soccer requires movements that involve a wide range of motion. For this reason flexibility training should be structured into a daily routine. The benefits of increased mobility and flexibility will be realized only through repetitions over time. It is easier to maintain flexibility than it is to develop it.

Along with providing increased range of motion, keeping your body flexible can help prevent the "injury bug" from appearing. Injury prevention is always a priority when training for competition. Flexibility becomes important for minimizing strains and pulls to muscles and ligaments when fatigue begins to cause a breakdown in your running and playing posture. Use flexibility exercises and stretches to maintain the integrity of your muscles, tendons, and ligaments during the rigors of game play. Afterward, cool-down routines using mainly static stretches (in which you hold the stretch position for a designated period) will help you recover.

General Flexibility Training   Lack of flexibility can affect many areas of fitness. Team-sport athletes must be able to change direction rapidly and absorb and produce force while under the stress of gravity. If you can create more range throughout your body, you will have more control (stabilization) while moving in space. Increased flexibility can also help you build strength through a larger range of motion. A large volume of strength training, especially nonfunctional strength training (like bodybuilding) will tend to have a shortening effect on your muscles and tendons, which can predispose you to strains and pulls. Using strength movements such as squatting, lunging, stepping, pressing, and pulling with increased range and multiple direction will have good transfer to the activity occurring on the field. Another performance benefit that can improve through increased flexibility is speed mechanics. Having range in your hip, knee, and ankle joints will increase your turnover rate (stride frequency) as well as the ability to lengthen your stride during top-speed sprinting.

Soccer-Specific Flexibility Training   Maintaining a full range of motion will help produce high-level performance on the soccer field. Movements involving striking the ball (kicking), sprinting, and jumping (heading) will be more fluid, efficient, and productive if training includes flexibility exercises on a daily basis. Because much of the game is reactive, increasing flexibility will also give you the ability to react quickly in multiple directions and stay a step ahead of your opponent. Because they cover a wide area on the field both horizontally and vertically, goalkeepers need good range of motion. Midfielders, who must possess and distribute the ball, have to jump, kick, reach, lean, and run around the field. Attack players can benefit from being mobile when they feint, dodge, and accelerate around, past, and among opponents.

Always remember that flexibility gains require a progressive, consistent routine.

BALANCE

Like all athletes, soccer players must maintain control and balance while reacting to the actions of the game. Players are in a constant battle with their opponents to gain (offensive) or reduce (defensive) playing space on the pitch. These battles, along with ground reaction forces (gravity, momentum, etc.), require that athletes perform under control with consistency. Using a mixture of both static drills to set the foundation and dynamic drills, you will begin to increase your ability to manage high-speed movements involving power, speed, and agility. Incorporating balance training with a few drills can be a small part of your total conditioning program that will provide big dividends in competition.

General Balance Training As mentioned earlier, to develop foundational control, soccer players should use mainly static, or nonmoving, balance training. This training stimulates the muscles to stabilize in a coordinated manner involving the whole body to maintain the center of mass and keep you from getting out of balance. The main emphasis here is to statically control movements for which you can later increase tempo or speed while maintaining balance. An example of this is stepping down off a stair or box and holding the landing on one foot. This exercise can be developed to the point of actually hopping off one foot to the other with high velocity and still keeping control upon landing.

Soccer-Specific Balance Training As you improve your foundational body control (holding positions without losing control) in conjunction with developing core strength (posture, hip and leg strength), your balance emphasis should move to high-speed functional drills that mimic the pace of the game. Remember, soccer is played in a reactive environment that is unpredictable. Controlling your center of mass in active situations requires good core strength and proprioception that by definition provide a sense of the body's position in space by responding to stimuli from within the body. In other words, you are trying to keep yourself from losing control. Situations such as feinting an opponent with the ball, winning a 50/50 ball in the air, and striking the ball with precision all demand that you be able to move while under control.

TOTAL-BODY STRENGTH

One area that soccer players tend to neglect is strength development. Years ago, soccer teams relied on general strength only, which they developed through practice and game play. There was never any emphasis on soccer-specific strength. Today's players are bigger, stronger, and more talented than ever. Technological and scientific research advancements have helped push training to new levels in the development of the total player, including strength. More coaches and players understand the importance of

Strength and power are critical for many of the moves and actions required in the game, including changing direction and diving.

developing strength to increase performance and diminish injury rates. In contrast to earlier times, the 2006 German national World Cup team even committed to using a performance coach while preparing for the tournament, which helped them succeed through the final game.

General Strength Training Developing strength that will transfer to competition is an important aspect in all of athletics. However, many athletes confuse strength training with bodybuilding or powerlifting types of training. Where bodybuilding and traditional resistance training fail is that they tend to isolate sections of the body and not train the movement patterns that soccer players must demonstrate in competition. Athletic-type strength training, which this book emphasizes, is a functional approach to total-body development. Using a solid core foundation that links the upper and lower body, the athlete gains balance, muscle–joint integrity, and power. Simply stated, the purpose of strength training is to elevate all aspects of performance.

Soccer-Specific Strength Training In the game of soccer, the demand for strength can change at a moment's notice throughout the 90 minutes of game time. The game is filled with awkward physical challenges while backpedaling, shuffling, diving on the ground, and quickly getting up to make the play. For the soccer player, high-intensity resistance training that recruits fast-twitch muscle fibers will pay dividends to the skills required in the game. Fast-twitch fibers are recruited when you need quick, fast, and explosive movement. These fibers have a limited blood supply, causing them to fatigue quickly, but they are able to perform when short, brief, high-powered movement is necessary. Movements that are explosive (i.e., require power) activate fast-twitch muscles. Exercises such as dumbbell power cleans and dumbbell jump squats fit into this category. Circuit training helps with conditioning during the competition phase of training and builds work capacity when starting a new off-season training phase. Kicking, acceleration, and change-of-direction movements should be developed through high-speed resistance training techniques.

Soccer must also be considered a contact sport. Players are constantly battling for the ball, position, and space. Developing lean body mass will help you withstand the physical collisions and cushion ground contact during the game. Improved body composition will keep you fit and improve muscle contraction, both concentrically (shortening the muscle) and eccentrically (lengthening the muscle).

POWER

In the game of soccer, a player's development of explosive power can lead to a great display of athleticism on the pitch. Many players possess strength or speed, but the combination of the two is what can separate the exceptional from the ordinary. It can also give you the competitive edge that is sought after by many.

General Power Training Explosive movement should be emphasized by athletes, like soccer players, to elicit fast, reactive training results usable in a game. By combining strength and power training, players will increase their ability to generate force in basic movements like sprinting, jumping, and cutting. Using jumping, hopping, and bounding as well as power throws in your program will help form the total-body power foundation. This quality will give you the confidence to perform at higher levels of play as well as transform your game into championship caliber.

Soccer-Specific Power Training As mentioned, soccer is a display of high-powered maneuvers of sprinting, changing direction, leaping, and kicking strength. Through total-body power training, soccer players can increase their speed of play and elevate the athletic qualities necessary for success with the individual duels that occur on the pitch. You will notice that the quality of your soccer skills begin to show lightning-quick pace. Kicking distance and strength will improve, jumping ability will be elevated, and racing past your opponent will become easier. Increasing your power with the help of drills found in this book will help you to experience how this quality can dominate your performance in the match.

SPEED

One of the top commodities in any sport is speed, which is the ability to get from one point to another as fast and efficiently as possible. This takes good sprinting mechanics with a good stride frequency (how fast you can get your legs to move), combined with increased stride length and total-body strength to generate powerful force on each takeoff. You may be wondering why a soccer player would need proper mechanics to run fast in a straight line, when soccer is played in random directions. Learning how to run correctly and efficiently can increase your efficiency during the game.

General Speed Training As mentioned, total-body strength and flexibility create a foundational platform to increase leg turnover (frequency) and the production of force against the ground on each step. Drills that incorporate tempo and rhythm help coordinate running mechanics and encourage the use of proper stride rates to ensure efficient running in top-speed situations. Speed development should be part of your general training program to produce positive results in competition.

Soccer-Specific Speed Training Speed is a valuable tool at any position on the field, except perhaps for goalkeepers. Once your running mechanics are correct, you can begin to develop the specific speed that will benefit your position. Forwards and wing players can use efficient running to win a loose ball from the opponent. Increased speed is a high premium for defenders, allowing them to erase bad positioning during the game. Setting the attack with speed gives midfield players the advantage that can change the game in an instant. As you progress in general speed development, incorporate specific drills to increase your confidence.

AGILITY

Coordination while reacting to what is happening on the field and doing so without delay is the objective of agility training. The ability to move quickly and under control can make a difference in competition and should be a major part of soccer fitness. Many great players from Mia Hamm to Ralehendino have developed a great first step to accelerate past the competition or change direction without hesitation. Training these qualities will bring your game to new heights.

General Agility Training Athletes in any sport can benefit from a quicker first step to gain an advantage when making the play. Good reaction time and the ability to stop and change direction quickly are also athletic qualities that aid in making the big play in competition. Agility training can help improve these skills.

Agility training can be as simple as jumping rope or as involved as partner mirroring drills, but the focus is always the same—to train at a fast rate, or game speed. Being able to "stop on a dime" requires developing game-speed intensity, functional strength, and balance, and controlling your center of gravity.

Soccer-Specific Agility Training It is easy to see why the ability to move quickly, efficiently, and under control enhances soccer performance. A striker's ability to maneuver around and accelerate past the defender increases her chances of scoring goals. Likewise, a defender who must backtrack to pick up trouble at the goal or a keeper who must make a split-second decision to make a save can benefit from agility drills. This book focuses on learning basic footwork patterns, together with stopping mechanics and both programmable and reaction-type drills, to give you a jump start on soccer quickness.

ENDURANCE

Sport conditioning should involve more than simply lining up and running sprints until total fatigue sets in. When endurance training for conditioning, most team-sport athletes obtain energy from all three energy sources (systems): stored energy for brief and explosive movements, recycled lactic acid for periods of intermediate length, and oxygen over the long term. To build an effective conditioning plan, soccer players should evaluate fitness demands in the context of what the sport requires, its time parameters, and the specific position's energy needs. Not all positions require a high percentage of aerobic conditioning. The objective is to condition for the way you play.

The energy systems used to maintain endurance on the field should be trained through a well-planned conditioning program.

General Endurance Training As mentioned, athletes can draw energy for performance from three basic sources: stored glycogen in the muscles, lactic acid, and oxygen. Aerobic training (with oxygen) has been part of conditioning training for many years. Most protocols call for training to elevate heart rate and develop the ability to use oxygen efficiently during sustained exercise. This is appropriate for certain athletic tasks (distance running, rowing, swimming). Most team sports, however, involve intense, repetitive movements with various rest intervals dispersed throughout. Conditioning should reflect this type of format. Speed endurance training uses the anaerobic energy system (without oxygen) to develop the athlete's ability to perform the intense, short, explosive bursts used in competition. This is accomplished through sprint intervals of various distances and intensities. Such training provides the sport-specific conditioning for keeping you fit, while mimicking gamelike intensity. I find that a solid sprint interval program will also increase most athletes' aerobic capacity enough to at least maintain a high value.

Soccer-Specific Endurance Training No matter where you play on the field, you will benefit from anaerobic speed endurance training. Video analysis of soccer game play has shown that soccer is a combination of sprinting, walking, jogging, backpedaling, and shuffling. All of these movements are performed at various intensities and for various lengths of time. Slow, methodical jogging or distance running will not transfer to the game and can even diminish acceleration and explosiveness. To positively condition for soccer, use the plan from this book to develop a conditioning base and stay at a high intensity level throughout the game.

Now that you understand the physical components of soccer, let's evaluate your current level of fitness for soccer. The next chapter will give you the tools to test and analyze your current strengths and weaknesses in each of the areas mentioned in this chapter.

Chapter 2

Assessing Soccer Fitness

There's a saying: Before you choose which direction to go, you first need to know where you are. That's the purpose of this chapter—to determine where you are in your journey toward soccer fitness. Only then can you set sensible fitness goals and use the exercises and drills throughout this book to achieve those goals. Certainly, observing or self-assessing soccer performance during practices and competition is useful, but to gather objective fitness information that you can act on, you must evaluate through testing.

Using this chapter, athletes and their coaches can test fitness to identify strengths and weaknesses that may affect performance. If possible, conduct baseline fitness tests at the start of the season, with checks at the midpoint and end of each competitive season. This will help you identify any drop-off in fitness that could erode performance on the field. The goal is to make regular testing easy to integrate into busy competition schedules so it is a key part of your comprehensive training plan.

Assessment results are not only valuable in predicting performance on the field, but also strong motivators for athletes to improve fitness. For this reason, coaches should share these results with their players. Through the years, I have seen many test batteries used to evaluate fitness—some useful and some less so. To judge the reliability of any test in jump-starting success on the field, answer the following questions:

- **Does the test measure what it's supposed to?** The tests you select should give you the basic information you are seeking. Measuring a standing broad jump will quickly tell you if your lower body has explosive strength, whereas the 20-yard shuttle run will measure quickness in a flash. If the test is not giving you the expected information, make sure the test, the testing environment, and testing protocols being executed are appropriate.

- **Will you be able to perform the test consistently?** To accurately compare and judge results, you must be able to perform the test the same way every time. Be conscious of timing methods, testing surfaces, type of shoes, and weather.
- **Is the test simple and clear?** The test should be easy to arrange and administer and have concise instructions.
- **Why are you testing?** Pinpoint your decision to evaluate. Whether your plan is to measure general fitness or specific skills or to check progress, customize your battery of tests to fit your personal needs.

Anson Dorrance, the legendary women's soccer coach at the University of North Carolina, believes in evaluating and ranking everything his team does—even practice drills. By doing so, he has been able to systematically improve the performance of his players, leading to championship results on the field. His assessment program is tailored to the program's particular needs. Likewise, for your assessment plan to meet your personal goals and fit within your training plan, it should meet your specific needs. For example, if you feel you are losing a step when you try to sprint past your opponent, evaluate your acceleration through the 30-meter sprint test to find any flaws (you would look at the time of your first 10 meters to evaluate your starting speed).

When organizing your test battery, follow these steps:

1. Understand and list the fitness demands of soccer.
2. Choose the tests that can evaluate these demands.
3. List the tests in the order they should be performed. This should be based on which tests will make the most muscular demands. For example, the test requiring the most endurance should be performed last.
4. Decide when to test. This will depend on your current phase of training or competition.
5. Perform the tests.
6. Collect and analyze scores with a coach or fitness trainer.
7. Use analyzed information to develop or adapt your training plan.

Table 2.1 shows a sample of a test battery I like to use to gather information on a soccer player's total fitness profile. This sample battery shows the most appropriate number of tests to execute as well as test descriptions and how each test relates to the game of soccer. Instructions for these tests are given in this chapter, along with other tests to choose from.

Table 2.1   Sample Fitness Test Battery

Test	Target fitness area	Soccer application
7-by-30-meter sprint test	Acceleration, anaerobic endurance, sprint efficiency	Sprint quality and recovery
Beep test	Anaerobic endurance	Sprint quality late in the game
Countermovement vertical jump test	Lower-body power, core strength, coordination	Kicking, sprinting, heading, cutting
Illinois agility test	Acceleration, agility	Cutting ability, body control, change of direction
Myrland hurdle under test	Dynamic flexibility, core strength	Dynamic balance, strength, range of motion
Total-body power throw with medicine ball	Total-body power	Explosive movements during competition

FIELD TESTS

At the University of North Carolina we conduct the following field tests twice a year. They provide an overview of players' current fitness levels from one year to the next and help pinpoint specific needs for each player. All of these tests can be performed with minimal equipment, on or near the field.

7-by-30-Meter Sprint Test

The 7-by-30-meter sprint endurance test is designed to be used on the field with players wearing soccer boots. This test evaluates sprint endurance, which is crucial to most positions in soccer. The athlete must be able to recover between efforts, which mimics game situations. It consists of seven 30-meter sprints, run as fast as possible, with a 25-second recovery interval that involves jogging back to the starting point. Ideally, the test should be timed with an electronic timing device, but a handheld stopwatch can give you a time that can be informative (it is usually 0.3 sec. slower than an electronic device).

Objective: Evaluate anaerobic power and endurance, sprint efficiency, and recovery ability.

Equipment: Stopwatch, six 12-inch (30 cm) cones or markers

Procedure: Warm up properly using an active stretching technique. The field surface should be level and free of obstructions. A wet surface can be hazardous to starting, as well as to slowing down when crossing the finish line. Begin the test 2 meters behind the designated starting line. The timer or start-timing beam begins as you cross the starting line. This ensures that you don't false start or trip the sensor too soon. On a "Go" command or whistle, sprint 30 meters past the finish line and slow down as soon as possible. Upon crossing the finish line, jog back to the starting line, with any remaining rest time (25 sec.) used to recover and reset at the start. The timer then gives a 5-second warning before the start of the next run.

Evaluation: We like to measure two factors using this test:

1. **Fastest time.** This is your straight-ahead speed (acceleration to top speed) as well as your fastest 10-meter acceleration, which is timed by a separate timer during the same run interval.

2. **Speed-velocity drop-off.** This is the difference between your fastest sprint and your slowest sprint, which tests anaerobic endurance. A small difference in drop-off indicates a fit athlete. The following equation is used to calculate drop-off:

$$\text{Drop-off} = \frac{\text{Slowest speed (time)} - \text{Fastest speed (time)}}{\text{Slowest speed (time)}} \times 100$$

Be sure to finish through the 30-meter mark to ensure an accurate time and drop-off rate. Each 30-meter sprint should be close to the top speed you can run for that distance. A scorekeeper should be placed at the finish line to record your score. The timer should also be at the starting area to announce rest periods.

Beep Test (Bangsbo Yo-Yo Intermittent Recovery)

This test is the result of research done by Jens Bangsbo, a Danish exercise scientist. This test indicates your ability to recover between bouts of intense work. It is performed with the use of an auditory signal (using a prerecorded CD) at intervals during the 40 meters (20 meters out, 20 meters back) covered on each test level. You follow a recorded set of instructions during the test. This recording can be played over a public address (PA) system at a field or stadium or on a portable player. A clear, dry, level space of 50 meters needs to be available. A 20-meter distance should be marked with a starting point and return. Scores are listed as "meters covered" along with the final speed level reached (the corresponding speed for each distance covered).

Objective: Measure anaerobic and muscular endurance with recovery ability.

Equipment: Beep test CD, two 12-inch (30 cm) cones or markers, portable CD player. This test requires a CD of the beep test because of the audio signal necessary to advance the test. The CD can be purchased through numerous coaching Web sites.

Procedure: The test begins with a start signal (beep), at which point you sprint 20 meters, stop, and return 20 meters to the starting point before the next beep. As you progress, the speed of each level increases, so you have to maintain an intense pace to keep from being eliminated. A short (10 sec.) rest period occurs after each interval. You will receive one warning when you miss your first level. The next miss eliminates you from the test.

Evaluation: The final score is determined by the total distance covered when exiting the test (each level totals 40 meters). Well-trained male soccer players can cover 2,000 to 2,300 meters. Some top female players exceed 1,800 meters, which represents an exceptional fitness level. The minimum standard for players at high levels should be around 1,000 meters.

Countermovement Vertical Jump Test

We administer this test on the field with the other field tests. There are two equipment options for setup: using a Vertec measuring apparatus (touch points on a vertical standard that are used in a number of sport testing events) or making marks on a designated wall near the field, such as an equipment storage building. The wall is more restrictive because you must stand close to it during the jump.

Objective: Measure and evaluate lower-body power, core strength, and coordination.

Equipment: Designated wall area or Vertec measuring device, marker or chalk

Procedure: The assigned jumping area should be clear of obstacles to ensure safe landings. Set the Vertec standard according to your height, so that when standing flat-footed you can reach up and touch a minimal number of vanes. (If using the wall method, the markings should reflect this same height.) This touch point represents your standing reach. Once the preliminary touch point is established, you can reuse this mark when further tests are administered in the future.

To begin the countermovement jump, position yourself directly under the Vertec with your feet in a parallel stance. Squat down to load your legs; then quickly jump up, extending your body vertically (figure 2.2, *a-b*). Your arms swing up forcefully to help aid in maximal power. Reach and touch the highest point possible. This represents your jump height. When using the wall method, make sure to eliminate any drifting into the wall that would stop your jumping momentum (figure 2.2, *c-d*). A chalk mark on the wall measures the jump height. The score is calculated by subtracting the standing reach from the jump touch score. For example, if your standing reach is 88 inches (224 cm) and your jump touch score is 120 inches (305 cm), then your test score would be 32 inches (120 − 88 = 32, or 305 − 224 = 81 cm). If using the wall method, just measure the distance between the start and jump heights to get the score.

Evaluation: This jump touch score can be useful to athletes and coaches as a quick measurement of power throughout the training year, to quantify off-season training, and to check power loss during the competitive season. The score can be compared to the athlete's previous scores to show improvement.

Figure 2.2   Countermovement vertical jump test: *(a-b)* load and jump using the Vertec method and *(c-d)* start height measurement and jump using the wall method.

Illinois Agility Test ⊙ 𝔻𝕍𝔻

Objective: Evaluate athletic acceleration, change of direction, and body control.

Equipment: Eight 12-inch (30 cm) cones, stopwatch

Procedure: This test should be performed on a nonslick surface such as grass or artificial turf. Eight cones are arranged in a 10-by-10-yard square with four cones set at the corners and the other four set halfway (5 yd.) in a weave pattern, as shown in figure 2.1. A timer should stand at the finish area.

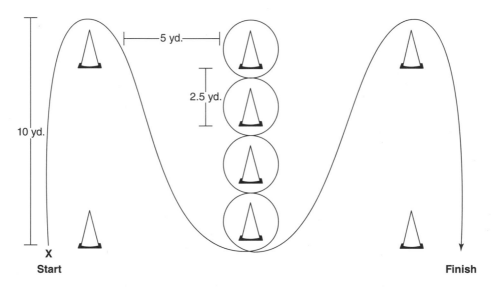

Figure 2.1   Illinois agility test.

To begin the test, position yourself at the designated starting cone lying facedown, your head even with the cone. Your hands and feet are raised off the ground in a stationary position. Start the test by getting off the ground quickly and accelerating to the top corner cone. After making a quick turn around the cone, again accelerate to the middle set of cones and perform a weave-type run up and back. At this point, reaccelerate to the farthest corner cone, make another turn, and sprint through the finish line. Two trials should be allowed, starting the test from both sides to compare right and left turning efficiency.

Evaluation: A successful run (less than 15 sec. for women and 14 sec. for men) indicates that you have the ability to move in a well-coordinated, explosive manner. A low score (greater than 16 sec. for women and 15 sec. for men) points to a need to develop core strength and acceleration/ reacceleration techniques. Drills such as plyometrics (jumps, hops, and bounds) and practicing starting and stopping quickly on command will help increase your performance on the Illinois agility test.

WEIGHT ROOM TESTS

The following tests evaluate the general components of athletic fitness and are useful in designing your off-season training. I like to administer these tests in a weight room or performance training area for preseason training as well as for progress checks throughout the season.

Flexibility Tests

The following tests subjectively measure your total-body flexibility. Flexibility fitness testing should be approached dynamically, not in a static manner. Think of your movements on the field—you need 360 degrees of movement! These tests can be used to quickly evaluate your top-to-bottom flexibility in motion.

Overhead Squat

Objective: Measure total-body (shoulder, spine, hip, knee, ankle) flexibility.

Equipment: A lightweight 7- to 8-foot (2 to 2.4 m) stick (PVC pipe, wood, or broomstick)

Figure 2.3 Overhead squat.

Procedure: The test should be done in low-cut socks or barefoot, so that the evaluator can clearly see foot and ankle position. Take a stance that is slightly wider than shoulder width and hold the stick overhead with a wide grip, elbows locked out. The stick should be in line with your shoulder bones. Maintaining this position will be a key observation point when evaluating the exercise. Squat down by flexing your ankles, knees, and hips to the lowest possible position (figure 2.3). Then return to the starting position keeping the stick overhead. Perform a series of 10 squats while a partner observes any deviations in posture (stiffness, loss of balance, lack of coordination) during the descent or ascent of each squat. These limitations should be addressed through a comprehensive flexibility routine that can be performed as part of a warm-up and or cool-down routine.

Evaluation: The following is a checklist for evaluating the overhead squat test. Use the answers to these questions to evaluate what areas of your body need attention. Perform stretches from chapter 3 that correspond to these focus points.

- Do your feet stay flat? (The heels should not rise during the descent of the squat.) If not, spend time stretching the calves and ankles.
- Do your knees move in or out when squatting down? (Your knees should not move too far in or out during the squat.) This indicates tightness in the adductors (groin area) as well as weak deep hip musculature.
- What is the position of your lower back? (Your posture should not deviate by rounding or arching too much.) Focus on stretching the hip flexors and psoas (deep hip muscles) and strengthening the abdominal and erector back muscles for stability.
- Do your arms come forward during the squat? If they do, this reflects tight shoulder and upper-back musculature.
- Does your head drop forward during the movement? If so, it indicates tightness in the shoulders and neck.

Myrland Hurdle Under Test

This test was developed by Steve Myrland, a sports performance coach with Myrland Sports Training in Wisconsin; Bill Knowles, an athletic trainer and rehab specialist with iSport Training in Vermont; and Vern Gambetta, a conditioning expert who has worked with players from the developmental levels to the elite national and pro soccer teams. It requires a standard adjustable track hurdle or a Smart-Hurdle made by Beacon Athletics. A measurement of your leg length from the crest of your hip bone to the floor is used to set the hurdle, as well as individualize the test.

Objective: Evaluate lower-body mobility, dynamic balance, and core strength and control.

Equipment: Adjustable track hurdle or Smart-Hurdle, measuring tape

Procedure: Set the hurdle so that the crossbar is perpendicular to a measured line on the floor. This line is the measurement of your leg length. The midpoint of the crossbar should divide your measured leg length. For example, if your leg length is 40 inches (102 cm), then place the crossbar at 20 inches (51 cm). At this point, you can now align yourself (if moving left to right) with your right foot starting at your leg length (40 in.) according to the measured line on the floor. The adjustable hurdle height should be set at a starting height of 30 inches (75 cm).

Figure 2.4   Myrland hurdle under test.

Start the hurdle test by moving left to right, stepping with your inside foot (left) under and through the center of the hurdle without making contact with your body (figure 2.4). A countermovement back to the starting point while anchoring the opposite foot completes one level of the test. This process continues while the hurdle is lowered another 3 inches (8 cm) after each successful attempt, until you make contact with the crossbar. Record the lowest mark and note any differences between right and left movements.

Evaluation: If you cannot lower your body below the first level (first locking hole on the hurdle uprights) without touching the crossbar, it is a good indicator that you have tightness and restrictions in movement, namely your hamstrings, hips, and lower back. You should focus more attention on stretching these areas.

Strength, Power, and Balance Tests

The following tests measure overall strength. Most of these are endurance tests, relating directly to game scenarios in which strength movements are repeated over and over again. These tests are useful for pretraining and pre- and postseason evaluations. They can also be of use for athletes who lack training experience using only their body weight as the resistance. They offer a functional assessment of athletic strength, looking at posture and core strength as they relate to soccer performance. These tests use basic equipment found in most gyms.

Single-Leg Squat

Soccer, like most team sports, is played while moving off one leg onto the other (sprinting, heading, kicking, changing direction). The ability to control single-leg movements and combine them with explosive power will be an advantage during game play. This screening quickly offers feedback on limitations of the left or right leg.

Objective: Evaluate total-body control, dynamic balance, and core strength.

Equipment: Clear, open space on a field or floor, tape or chalk

Procedure: Make a 2- to 3-foot (60 to 90 cm) line (with tape or chalk) on the floor to use as a starting mark. Start by standing and balancing on one leg on the line, with both hands on your hips. You should be able to hold this position without falling or touching the opposite foot to the ground. Bend the test leg at the ankle, knee, and hip to get down to the lowest possible position. The opposite leg rotates out in front while keeping the knee locked (figure 2.5). Perform the movement without touching this leg to the ground.

Figure 2.5   Single-leg squat.

Evaluation: Notice whether the balancing leg's heel maintains contact with the ground during the movement or pops up to reveal limited range of motion in the ankle. Also, consider the depth of the squat and compare differences in balance between the right and left legs. If deviations occur during the squat, introduce both ankle and hamstring stretches and perform single-leg squats with the nonstanding leg either reaching forward or backward.

Incline Body Row

This test can be used as an alternative to the standard pull-up exercise, especially for female athletes when developing strength.

Objective: Evaluate upper-body and core strength endurance.

Equipment: Power rack or adjustable bar standard with a standard weightlifting bar

Procedure: Use a basic power rack or open platform that has an adjustable standard. Set the standard so that when you are flat on your back (supine) with your arms straight and holding the bar, your body does not touch the ground (hanging position). This will depend on your arm length. Once the bar height is established, position yourself under the bar to begin the test. Use an overhand grip and place the rest of your body in a straight line with your heels touching the ground (figure 2.6a). I ask athletes to visualize that their body is a 2-by-4-inch board so that they maintain a tight posture throughout the movement.

A timer gives you a start command, at which point you have 1 minute to repeatedly pull yourself up so your chest nearly touches the bar (figure 2.6b). We typically see above-average scores of 30 or more repetitions for female players and 45 or more repetitions for males.

Figure 2.6   Incline body row.

Evaluation: As mentioned before, limited upper-body strength for female players seems to be the norm, so attention can be spent on a basic strength program, even during competition cycles of the year. Exercises such as various pulling movements—pull-downs, pull-ups, and weighted rows—will improve upper-body strength and increase performance on the incline body row test for both male and female players.

Total-Body Power Throw With Medicine Ball

This test is a functional means to evaluate your explosive strength. Designate a throwing area that is open and free of obstacles. Unless you are on an outside field, a ceiling height of at least 20 feet (6 m) will be needed to allow enough clearance during the throw.

Objective: Measure total-body power (speed strength).

Equipment: Medicine ball (2 kg [4.4 lb.] for females, 3 kg [6.6 lb.] for males), measuring tape

Procedure: Begin by standing behind a start line with your feet shoulder-width apart. Raise the medicine ball up to chest height, placing your hands on the ball as if throwing a basketball chest pass. Squat slightly down to load your hips and legs (figure 2.7a) and quickly extend your body, feeling the movement from your feet up through your hands as the ball is released. On release, push the ball up and out as far as possible (figure 2.7b). This explosive movement should cause you to leave the ground briefly, which may cause you to land over the starting line. This is perfectly fine because, during the release, we are looking for maximum power value with limited deceleration from the body.

Evaluation: Take two or three attempts after a good warm-up. Each throw should be measured from the starting line to the point where the ball hits the ground, to the nearest 6 inches (15 cm). Typically, above-average throws for females are over 25 feet (8 m), and for males are over 35 feet (11 m).

Figure 2.7   Total-body power throw with medicine ball.

Body Plank Hold

The body plank hold is an endurance-based, subjective measurement of core strength. I use this to evaluate the early training state of our athletes.

Objective: Subjectively evaluate total-body core strength.

Equipment: Clear, open space on a field or floor

Procedure: Get down on the floor, in a prone position similar to that of doing a push-up. Bend your arms 90 degrees so your elbows are resting on the ground, directly under your shoulders. Your feet are flexed so that the only other contact points on your body are your toes (figure 2.8). During the test your hips and torso will remain elevated, forcing you to activate your core muscles.

Evaluation: Once you are stationary, time the plank hold for 1 minute and have someone observe you for any deviations from the starting position. The things to look for include dropping or elevating of the hips from the midline, shifting weight forward to the shoulders, or leaning to one side or the other. This test can also be used as part of a core strength workout.

Figure 2.8   Body plank hold.

Shark Skill Test

This test was designed by fitness scientists Matt Sherry and Mike Clark (thus **Sh**erry and Cl**ark**) of the National Academy of Sports Medicine to evaluate single-leg functional balance. It is a good way, along with the single-leg squat test, to evaluate your ability to support and actively move your body on one leg. The setup for the test begins with a temporary grid on a nonslick floor with nine 1-by-1-foot (30 by 30 cm) squares stacked together within a 3-by-3-foot (90 by 90 cm) square (figure 2.9). The center square is designated as the starting point for the test. A timer scores each trial.

8	1	2
7	Start X Finish	3
6	5	4

3 ft.

3 ft.

Figure 2.9 Grid setup for the shark skill test.

Objective: Measure single-leg functional balance.

Equipment: Floor tape or chalk, stopwatch

Procedure: To start the test, stand on the center square on one leg. (The test will be performed again using the other leg.) Your hands are placed on your hips throughout the test, and a 0.1-second deduction is applied to the final score each time your hands drop from this position. A deduction is also applied if you perform the test out of sequence (missing the appropriate box). Start the test by performing a series of single-leg hops, alternating from the center square to the other squares using a clockwise (right foot moving right) or counterclockwise (left foot moving left) pattern. The timer starts the clock on the first movement and stops it when you return to the center square after touching the last square in sequence.

Evaluation: Along with differences in time from the right to left foot, the timer can observe limitations in your range or balance. Usually your speed on this test dramatically increases just by practicing footwork and balance drills even for a short period of time.

Testing and evaluating can play an important part in keeping your training headed in the right direction. Use the tests that will give you the best feedback for your particular needs. Testing can be as simple as two or three drills that can be quickly executed and managed within your training routine. Challenge yourself by working to improve from your previous test scores. You can improve your fitness by applying the exercises and drills in each chapter of this book. Let's begin the process by discussing flexibility.

Chapter 3

Flexibility

Now that you are clearer about your current fitness level through assessment, you can begin to develop a training plan that can serve your specific needs. This chapter is the first of six chapters that provide drills and exercises designed to increase your performance in the various fitness components.

Flexibility is mainly the ability to move your body through a full range of motion. In soccer, being able to move and perform well in the wide array of positions that the body may go through during a match will help improve your game. This improvement can be anything from increasing your running stride to increasing the follow-through when driving the ball.

Conventional wisdom tells us that good flexibility means being able to statically touch your toes or perform a full split. To some degree this may have some value, but this is only a starting point for most athletes. Stretching should be a means to increase flexibility. Match play requires a combination of coordinated movements such as reaching, bending, leaning, and twisting that can only be improved through training. This means that along with static flexibility routines, you must spend time in dynamic flexibility routines that have rhythm and tempo. This is sometimes referred to as increasing mobility.

Flexibility should be part of all facets of training—from warm-up and cool-down and recovery to strength, power, and agility training. This section presents individual stretches and dynamic routines as well as yoga poses that will bring flexibility increases.

WARM-UP

Most exercise activity starts with a warm-up session, which typically involves some form of flexibility work. Athletes have used stretching for years to prepare the body for strenuous training or competition. The loosening and warming effect increases core temperature and decreases joint stiffness.

A warm-up generally includes a period of cardiovascular exercise (for example, jogging) to warm the muscles and then proceeds to stretching exercises to avoid straining or pulling muscles while performing. However, it is important to understand that just because you've stretched, you're not necessarily fully warmed up. Your warm-up should stimulate and activate the nervous system as well to get you ready for full-speed activity. The nervous system is what "turns on" the muscles to perform. Activating the nervous system puts it on alert that something more intense is about to happen. Muscle firing patterns and systematic coordination are enriched by placing a well-calculated warm-up period before activity. These warm-ups should mimic the general movements used on the field.

As stated before, soccer play involves explosive movements that occur randomly over an extended period of time. These movements can subject

©Human Kinetics

Flexibility not only helps prevent injury, it also allows a full range of motion for powerful movements.

the body to unusual bending, twisting, reaching, and pulling positions. Unprepared athletes extended past their limits can be subjected to strains, pulls, and other soft-tissue injuries. Likewise, strenuous training sessions take a toll on the body's range of motion. Increasing your mobility will improve mechanical tasks such as sprinting by allowing you to expend less energy; maintain coordination, balance, agility, and strength; and limit breakdown of movement range through fatigue. I like to use mobility drills as part of warm-ups and cool-downs, or even as part of the workout. Most athletes benefit from working the hips, ankles, and shoulders. These areas tend to lose range of motion through overuse during practice and training.

For many soccer players, warm-ups are an afterthought during practice and even competition. I've seen inexperienced players jog a few minutes, touch their toes, reach overhead, and start playing. This approach is a quick setup for injuries somewhere down the road. By devoting as little as 10 minutes to a daily routine, you can establish a flexibility foundation.

I like to use three basic stretching techniques to develop flexibility in athletes: *dynamic stretching, static stretching,* and *active stretching.* Dynamic stretching, used before practice or competition, is a combination of movement drills and stretching that stimulate and prepare the body for an increased workload. Dynamic stretching drills may remind you of the calisthenic drills used in physical education classes years ago (i.e., carioca, shuffling, jumping jacks). Static stretching, or "stretch and hold," has a soothing effect on the body and is beneficial after training or competition. This type of stretching is often misused prior to activity, putting athletes in a relaxed mode. Active stretching, also known as "contract and relax," is used as a recovery technique from heavy bouts of exercise. All three can be placed throughout all phases of training to increase flexibility. Table 3.1 shows flexibility categories and sample exercises to give purpose to your routine.

Table 3.1 Types of Flexibility Training

Category	Activity or stretch	Placement in session or competition
Dynamic stretches	Walking knee hug to lunge (see page 29)	Prepractice, precompetition
Mobility drills	Hurdle walk (see page 31)	Pre- and posttraining, during training
Static stretches	Side groin stretch (see page 36)	Posttraining, postcompetition
Active stretches (with partner)	Partner straight-leg hamstring stretch (see page 41)	Posttraining, postcompetition as recovery

DYNAMIC FLEXIBILITY ROUTINES

The routines outlined in this section will help you ready yourself for a training session or warm up for competition. The variations allow you to choose a plan according to the time you have available. Typically, routines range from 8 to 15 minutes in length. Routine I is 8 to 12 minutes long, and routine II is 12 to 15 minutes long. There is also an additional sequence within routine II for agility-type training sessions.

Dynamic Stretching Routine I

This is a basic routine for a quick snapshot warm-up for readiness when time is a factor (e.g., precompetition). Use an area that is 20 to 25 yards square.

1. Jog and backpedal back and forth continuously for 20 seconds (you can use the perimeter).
2. Side shuffle 20 yards and back using an alternating arm swing from overhead to across the chest.
3. Carioca (grapevine step) down and back; switch the lead leg on the way back to the starting point. The footwork sequence for the carioca step is: side step, crossover step, side step, and step behind the lead step.
4. Skip (use a forward, lateral, and backward style).
5. Backpedal.
6. Power skip (for height).
7. Squat jump, in place, × 3. Bend down by flexing the ankle, knee, and hip and explode up in the air as high as possible.
8. Four × 10-yard acceleration (2 × 75% speed, 1 × 85%, 1 × 95%). Accelerations should get faster progressively so that the last one is just under full speed.
9. Two × 2 lateral bounds to a 10-yard acceleration.
10. Squat jump × 2 to a 10-yard acceleration.

*For precompetition, add short-ball skills (one touch, two touches with short sprints) at the end of the warm-up.

Dynamic Stretching Routine II (long version, 20- to 30-yard distance)

This routine is for an extended prepractice warm-up. This routine should take 12 to 15 minutes. Refer to the drill descriptions at the end of the chapter.

1. Jog down and backpedal back for 20 seconds.
2. Jog with 4 or 5 toe-touch stretches (pause and stretch)—reach hands to feet.
3. Shuffle back to the starting point—side shuffle with arms reaching overhead.
4. Crossover stance hip stretch, jogging between stretches—figure four, with one leg over the balanced leg, and move the hips back.
5. Jog back to the starting point.
6. Walking knee hug to forward lunge—march, pulling knee to chest and step into a forward lunge.
7. Skip back to the starting point.
8. Marching leg swings—march, swinging legs up to arms extended overhead.
9. Single-leg support, reach for the ground—reach both arms to the ground while swinging one leg backward.
10. Alternating side lunge—alternate lead legs.
11. Spiderman crawl, side groin stretch (see stretch description).
12. Hurdle step forward and backward—hands on head, walk with a high knee step.
13. Shuffle.
14. Carioca (grapevine step).
15. Skip forward and backward.
16. Side skip.
17. Backpedal.
18. Power skip.
19. Three × 10-yard acceleration (increase speed each sprint).

Add these movement drills to the preceding routine for agility and change-of-direction preparation:

1. S runs forward and backward—run in a curve pattern.
2. Three-step "plant and cut"—run for 3 steps, and then alternate planting and cutting in the opposite direction.
3. Side bounds × 2 right and left—jump to the side off one leg to the other.
4. Run with 360-degree turn—run through a full turn.
5. Backpedal, turn, and run.

Post-Halftime Routine

Following an intermission period, you should give some attention to restarting the body for full-speed play. Because time is limited, a modified dynamic warm-up is appropriate, using a mixture of forward, backward, and lateral movements combined with jumping and sprinting. You should be allowed to create your own routine based on what gets you back in playing mode. Because you often have only 5 to 10 minutes available to warm up before the second half begins, you have to work quickly.

COOL-DOWN

Once your training session or competition has ended, your body needs to gradually cool down to a relaxed state to begin the recovery process. This is the time to use a combination of static and active stretches to balance out the stresses of training and competition. The amount of time needed will depend on how much time you played or how stressful the training session was. The majority of stretches in the cool-down routine are similar to those in the warm-up routines.

Cool-Down Routine

Once you have given yourself 5 to 10 minutes to relax, begin the cool-down with light jogging for a minute or two, and then use an open space of about 10 yards square.

1. Walk forward a few steps, stop, and reach for your feet (toe touch stretch)—repeat for 10 yards.
2. Turn around, walk back, and perform 4 or 5 crossover hip stretches—10 yards.
3. Walking knee hugs—10 yards.
4. Alternating side lunges—10 yards.
5. Alternating walking leg swings—10 yards.
6. Walking thigh stretch (holding foot behind)—10 yards.

When completed, perform 3 or 4 of the partner stretches listed later in this chapter.

MOBILITY DRILLS

The drills in this section are designed to promote suppleness throughout the body as a precursor to heavier training or as part of the workout itself. The goal here is to create functional movement using your body, the ground, and gravity. These drills can also be used as an extension of the dynamic stretches performed in warm-up for training by increasing the intensity of the warm-up.

Hurdle Walk ⊙ 📀

Line up a row of four adjustable hurdles at the lowest setting. Using a tall posture, walk over each hurdle, attempting to lift your knee to your armpit and bringing the bottom of your foot over the top of the hurdle. Try not to extend your lower leg as you step over the hurdle, creating less bend in the knee, because this will limit your ability to move fluidly. Perform the following variations to create a three-plane series of stretches (front, side, and rotational): forward with both feet over (a), alternating step forward, lateral step (b), and back step. Perform 2 sets of each movement.

Hurdle walk: (a) forward with both feet over; (b) lateral step.

Oregon Shift Drill ⓞ 𝐷𝑉𝐷

This drill, designed by Jim Radcliffe at the University of Oregon, really works the hips and groin. Take a wide stance and drop your hips as low as possible while keeping your back flat and head up. Hold on to two cones (12 in., or 30 cm) while leaning and shifting your weight, without lifting your feet, and place one cone on the ground as far to the side as you can. Repeat to the opposite side. Return to the middle position, lean to one side, and touch the top of the cone. Continue back and forth, touching the cones for 10 repetitions. Progress from no step to one, two, or multiple steps. Perform the same movement while placing the cone another one or two steps wider and using either one or two steps to reach and touch the cone.

Lunge and Reach

Stand tall with feet together. Begin by taking a long step forward, striking the ground with a heel-toe landing. As the foot makes contact, lean

and reach forward for the front toes, keeping your arms elongated. Pause for a count, and then push back to the starting position. Repeat three to five times for each leg. Add a lateral step (side step) and rotational step (turn and rotate on a 45-degree angle backward) to work in different planes. I sometimes add a light medicine ball to help increase the speed of movement and activate core musculature.

Overhead Squat

This exercise is intended to develop hip, knee, ankle, upper-back, and shoulder mobility as one coordinated movement. It can be performed as a warm-up or within a training session.

Stand with your feet parallel and wider than shoulder width. Hold on to a lightweight bar or broomstick using a wide grip and locking your arms. Lift the bar over your head. Squat down as low as possible while keeping the bar overhead. Be conscious of keeping your feet flat throughout the entire movement. Perform 2 or 3 sets of 10 repetitions. (See photo on page 17.)

CRAWLING PATTERNS

Crawling patterns not only develop mobility in the hips and shoulders, but also emphasize coordination, limb opposition, and core strength.

Use an open space where you can move on the ground for 10 to 15 yards. When performing these movements, pay attention to controlling your center core. Moving with your hips raised or sagging past the midline will not provide stability and support for your body in motion. The three basic crawling drills I use for training are the Spiderman crawl, walkouts, and low and slow carioca.

Spiderman Crawl

Start with your body in a push-up position on your hands and toes. Bring one foot up to the outside of the corresponding hand while attempting to place the elbow as close as possible to the ground, keeping the back knee off the ground. Repeat on the other leg by crawling forward on hands and feet. Perform 5 stretches on each leg, holding for 6 seconds.

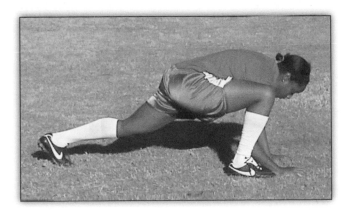

Walkout

Stand with your feet together and bend forward to place your hands on the ground. Gradually walk your hands out with short steps until they reach a point just past your head. This should put your body in a straight line position. While maintaining a tight core and straight legs, slowly walk your feet back up as close as you can to your hands. Repeat the sequence by walking your hands out again (6 repetitions).

Low and Slow Carioca

Take a wide stance with your feet wider than shoulder width. Place your hands on the ground and begin a basic carioca (grapevine) stepping pattern *(a)* while holding each step for 3 to 5 seconds. Try to keep your hips as low as possible and your head up, eyes looking forward. Continue for 16 steps (4 cycles), moving in both directions *(b)*.

STATIC STRETCHES

The following menu of stretches offers the basics for finishing off workouts or cool-down periods after a match. Hold each stretch for 20 to 30 seconds.

Prone Calf

Targets: Calves and ankle musculature

Starting from a push-up position on the ground, cross one leg over the other, transferring the weight onto the bottom foot. Attempt to press the heel of the bottom foot to the ground and hold. To attack a different angle, bend the bottom leg slightly and try to get the heel down to the ground.

Static Spiderman

Targets: Hamstrings, groin, glutes, and lower back muscles

Use the same starting position as in the Spiderman crawl: Begin in a push-up position and then bring one foot up past the hand of the same-side leg while keeping the back leg straight. Lower the elbow at the front leg down toward the ground, attempting to rest it on the ground inside the front leg. Hold the elbow as close to the ground as possible, keeping the back leg extended. Repeat with the opposite leg.

Wide-Stance Three-Position Reach

Targets: Lower back, groin, and hamstrings

Take an extra-wide stance. Attempt to bring your hands to the ground by leaning forward with your palms flat. Hold for 30 seconds. Continue the stretch, moving your hands to the right foot and then the left, with your head close to your knee.

Side Groin Stretch

Targets: Adductors and hamstrings

With your feet in a wide stance, shift your weight to one side, placing your hands on the ground inside of your feet. Work to keep both feet flat and feel the stretch on the side of the weight shift. Hold for 30 seconds.

Deep Forward Lunge Stretch

Targets: Hamstrings, glutes, and lower back

Step one leg far forward to a 90-degree bend. Bring your upper body forward, rounding your back, and reach for your front foot. Sit into the stretch and hold for 30 seconds. Add a torso rotation by turning your upper body to one side in an upright position as you continue to sit into the lunge. Take the arm of the front leg parallel to the ground and hold in a twisting position. Repeat on the other leg.

Standing Quadriceps Stretch

Targets: Quadriceps and hip flexors

Stand tall and hold one foot behind your back by bending your leg at the knee. If you have balance issues with this stretch, hold on to a partner's shoulder for support (or a wall, bench, or fence). Hold the position for 30 seconds.

Overhead Triceps Stretch

Targets: Triceps and latissimus dorsi

Stand with one arm bent at the elbow and raised at the side of your head. Reach over the top of your head with the opposite arm and hold the raised elbow. Pull the elbow back under control to a position just behind your head. Hold the stretch for 20 seconds. Repeat to the opposite side. To increase the intensity, lean your bent arm against a wall or barrier and sink your torso into the stretch.

Standing Reach and Side Bend

Targets: Upper back and shoulders

Stand tall with your feet together and bring both arms overhead. Extend your body to lengthen through your back and shoulders. Keep your feet grounded and balanced. Hold for 20 to 30 seconds. After the initial stretch is completed, take the stretch to both sides by bending at the waist. Hold the stretch for 20 seconds on each side.

Star Side Reach

Targets: Latissimus dorsi, lower back, and shoulders

Stand with your feet wide and pointed slightly out. Raise your arms out to the side, holding them parallel to the ground (this will form the five points of a star: head, arms, and legs). Attempt to lower yourself down one side without allowing your torso to rotate forward. Hold the stretch for 20 seconds. Come back to the center and lower to the opposite side.

Cross-Chest Shoulder Stretch

Targets: Shoulder and upper back

Stand with one arm extended across your chest. Hold on to the extended arm with the opposite arm and pull it into your chest. Hold for 30 seconds. Repeat to the opposite side.

Neck Static Stretch

Targets: Neck musculature and trapezius

Hold one side of your head with the opposite arm (e.g., right arm holding the left side of your head). Place the other arm behind your back. Gradually pull your head to the side, attempting to bring it as close as possible to your shoulder *(a)*. Hold for 20 seconds and repeat to the opposite side. Move back to the original side and grab the back of your head. Tuck your chin to your armpit and hold for 20 seconds *(b)*. In the final position, place your hand on your forehead and push back to a 45-degree angle *(c)*. Hold for 20 seconds.

Yoga Routine

Recently yoga and yogalike exercises have appeared more frequently in athletic workouts and cool-down periods to generate mobility throughout the body. They offer the added benefits of balance and body awareness. I have included four basic poses that I use to help increase range of motion. Hold the poses as long as you like while moving through the sequence.

Downward-facing dog: With your hands and feet in contact with the ground, form an upside-down V with your body *(a)*. Extend your back and bring your heels as close as possible to the ground with your head down and relaxed.

Upward-facing dog: Move from the previous position by bringing your hips to the ground and raising your upper torso off the ground with your arms locked *(b)*.

Child's pose: From the upward-facing position, raise your hips and sit back on your feet while reaching your arms out in front *(c)*. Keep your head down and relax.

Deep lunge with rotation: From a push-up position, bring one leg up into a lunge position with your hands on the ground. Sink your hips and then rotate your front leg up to a perpendicular position. Rotate your upper body toward your front leg, extending your arm upward in a straight line *(d)*. Hold the position and then repeat with the opposite leg.

Yoga poses: *(a)* Downward-facing dog, *(b)* upward-facing dog, *(c)* child's pose, and *(d)* deep lunge with rotation.

ACTIVE STRETCHES

The purpose of active stretches is to take advantage of the reciprocal inhibition principle of muscles. In this principle, contraction of the muscles opposite those being stretched will increase relaxation in the stretched muscles. For example, if you want to stretch your hamstrings, you would get your leg in a position to lengthen the back part (lying down with the leg straight up at 90 degrees). By using a partner to hold the leg in this static position, you would contract the front muscles of your leg (quadriceps) for a few seconds, trying to move your leg to the ground and allowing the receptors in the hamstrings (the target) to signal relaxation. Such a stretch allows you to stretch the target muscles past the starting point. Be conscious of knowing where your limit is on each stretch to avoid injury. You should feel tension, not pain. You can repeat several times and apply this technique to both upper- and lower-body areas. I use this type of stretching mainly postworkout or postcompetition.

Partner Straight-Leg Hamstring Stretch

Targets: Hamstrings

Start with your back on the ground and your legs extended. Your partner bends down in the front and positions herself on one knee, bringing the target leg up to rest on her shoulder. Your partner holds onto the leg by placing one hand on the foot and one on the knee of the target leg. Contract your thigh muscles (quadriceps) and attempt to push your leg to the ground. Hold the static contraction for 6 seconds. While relaxing, your partner should bring the target leg up higher to increase the stretch. Repeat the sequence two more times and then switch to the opposite leg.

Partner Knee-to-Chest Hamstring Stretch

Targets: Hamstrings

Lie on your back with your legs extended. Bring one knee to your chest as far as possible, while your partner positions herself in front, placing one hand on the knee and the other on the heel of your bent leg. While keeping your knee close to your chest, your partner resists the heel from moving to your backside (simulating a leg curl exercise). Hold the static stretch for 6 seconds, after which your partner extends your lower leg, keeping the knee close to your body. After repeating the sequence two more times, you should be able to extend your lower leg to your farthest position. Repeat the sequence on the opposite leg.

Partner Hip Flexor Stretch

Targets: Quadriceps and hip flexors

Lie facedown on the ground with your legs extended. Your partner bends down to the target-leg side and places one hand on your lower back while cradling your leg in a flexed-knee position. Attempt to bring your knee to the ground while your partner statically holds the position for 6 seconds. When you relax, your partner can extend your leg to a higher position and hold. Repeat the stretch on the other leg.

Partner Crossover Stretch

Targets: Lower back, glutes, deep hip muscles

Lie on your back with your arms extended out to the side. Cross one leg over the other while trying to keep your shoulders in contact with the ground. Your partner uses her foot to keep your straight leg from moving while placing one hand behind the bent knee and the other on the top of the shoulder opposite the bent leg. Your partner statically keeps the bent leg from rising upward for 6 seconds, after which she moves the leg closer to the ground. To increase the stretch intensity, raise your bent knee higher toward your armpit. Repeat a few times and switch legs.

Remember that stretching alone does not constitute a thorough warm-up. Stretching is important to flexibility, but a proper warm-up will also include active exercises, three-dimensional movement, and neuromuscular stimulation. An appropriate flexibility routine will give you the foundation on which to build speed, control, explosiveness, and strength.

Chapter 4

Balance

The ability to control the body in space is a valuable tool for an athlete in any high-speed sport. For soccer players, this control, or balance, is imperative during most aspects of the game. Whether you are tracking an offensive star player, landing after heading the ball, or dribbling past an opponent, good balance is crucial, especially when you consider the amount of contact involved in the game. Regardless of the position you play, you will appreciate a heightened awareness of your body in space.

Like flexibility training, balance training should be part of your conditioning foundation. It should begin with basic postural control that will help develop intrinsic core strength and stability. The ultimate goal of balance training, though, is to provide dynamic stability, or balance in motion, and optimum neuromuscular control (the ability to fire the appropriate muscles efficiently and without delay). In other words, you want to build a strong, well-coordinated base that supports rapid movements.

Balance training should be incorporated into the training of all the other components because it serves as the link between producing and reducing movement. Whether you're performing a strength move (single-leg squat), a plyometric jump (rotational jump), or planting and cutting on the field, your body must maintain control.

Helping you move and react without losing control is the job of the processing mechanisms in the brain that maintain a state of equilibrium. The body also calls on the proprioceptors (small receptors in the muscles, tendons, and ligaments) to respond to changes in body position, center of mass, and muscle length. These mechanisms can also be trained and improved to help your performance on the field. As they improve, your adjustments during game-speed situations will also become sharper and more efficient.

I have seen some athletes with limited training experience but good skill levels who have never turned on these balancing mechanisms during their early developmental years. So for them, consciously training control and balance is like turning on a switch that can elevate performance. Training balance throughout workouts can benefit the average player.

This being said, balance training doesn't need to be extensive. I've seen balance training taken to ridiculous levels, with athletes spending hours putting themselves in unusual training positions with every kind of equipment imaginable. Touching on a few points during each workout session is adequate—either in the warm-up, a weight room session, or an agility workout. For example, after an active warm-up period you might perform 1 or 2 sets of single-leg squats and touches to activate the proprioceptors in your ankles, knees, and hips. This, along with the actual warm-up, is a good way to stimulate the nervous system into total-body readiness. Increase the difficulty of the drill by closing one eye, or have a partner nudge your body during each repetition. You can see positive results with as little as 5 or 10 minutes of balance training daily.

It is also worth mentioning that improving balance can supply structural stability to ankle and knee joints. This is important to all soccer players because of the increased risks of ACL (anterior cruciate ligament) tears. Many players concentrate on balance improvements only when the injury

©Jean Marie Hervio/FLASH PRESS/Icon SMI

Because many situations involve body contact with other players, good balance and body control are important attributes to hone.

has already occurred and it becomes part of the rehabilitation process. This does not mean that balance training will eliminate any chance of injury, but by introducing balance awareness to the joints, you create a mental library of unstable positions that will help you to withstand the reactive forces during dynamic situations in competition. Once you have established a basic foundation, keep the drills as part of a maintenance phase of training during the season.

BALANCE TRAINING PROGRESSION

The key to designing a balance training program is to challenge your comfort zone and build from one session to the next to extend those parameters. The menu of drills should reflect posture, control, and dynamic stability. Once you observe or feel comfortable with static posture, start expanding your exercises and drills to increase the demand for dynamic control. The single-leg squat and touch or reach is a great starting point from which to discover your balance limitations. As mentioned in chapter 2, the single-leg squat can be tested early in training as a general indicator of control and stability on one leg.

A variety of equipment is available to challenge this component, including balance discs, boards, and foam pads. However, try to keep your drills simple and applicable to soccer. As mentioned before, training sessions can become too equipment driven. Consider progressing gradually with subtle changes. Gravity and momentum can even be used as a way to dynamically fuel your training. For example, body-weight exercises, including the single-leg squat and reach or the single-leg hop and hold, are a great way to emphasize body control with gravity and momentum serving as a stimulus. Table 4.1 on page 48 provides a list of balance training variables with examples of basic as well as advanced exercises.

I suggest that you choose a balance drill and start practicing it slowly. After you've mastered this, progress to performing the movement faster. These subtle changes in the drill will increase total-body control and help you develop proficiency during movement.

When performing the balance drills, move to an advanced mode only when improvement is observable. There is no value to trying to hold a posture on a foam pad or walking beam if you are unable to hold it on stable ground. By training the neuromuscular system and the proprioceptors with a variety of stimuli, you will create an environment that will improve your performance.

Let's look at the basic single-leg squat and reach to understand the training sequence. Initially, you would perform the exercise with maximum control and statically hold the bottom squat position for several seconds. When you have mastered control, you can add speed, tempo, and resistance as well as unstable surfaces. Instead of holding the squat, you would quickly move up and down to increase the tempo as well as the difficulty.

The same process would be applied to developing your jump through plyo-metric training. A squat jump could progress from jumping and holding the landing to jumping in multiple directions without shoes or in sand. Table 4.2 takes the single-leg squat and reach exercise through a training progression from the basic movement to the advanced stage. The key is not to get too comfortable with the stimulus and the drill. Remember that what happens on the field is mostly reactionary and unexpected.

Table 4.1   Training Variables for Balance

Basic level	Advanced level	Variation examples
Slow	Fast	Slow: Hopping on one foot, side to side, while sticking the landing Fast: Hopping on one foot continuously, counting the number of foot contacts in 10 seconds
Stable	Unstable	Stable surface: Single-leg squat and reach on floor Unstable surface: Single-leg squat and reach on a foam pad
Static	Dynamic	Static: Squat on BOSU ball, holding the squat for 5 seconds Dynamic: Two-footed jump on the BOSU ball with a squat
Body weight	Resistance	Body weight: Step-up, overhead reach, and hold Resistance: Dumbbell step-up, overhead press, and hold
Eyes open	Eyes closed	Eyes open: Single-leg Romanian deadlift, both eyes open Eyes closed: Single-leg Romanian deadlift, eyes closed on the way down

Table 4.2   Sample Progression for Single-Leg Squat and Reach Balance Exercise

Basic—Easy
Body-weight single-leg squat and reach (reach out), 2 × 10 reps each leg, hold the bottom position for 5 seconds

Intermediate—Moderate
Single-leg squat and reach with weighted vest (10-20% of body weight) and eyes closed

Advanced—Hard
Single-leg squat and reach, barefooted and on an unstable surface (pad, mat, or beam)

BALANCE DRILLS

Here are some drills and exercises that can help you improve stability and control. Each drill includes a beginning and advanced level as well as a soccer-specific tweak.

Single-Leg Squat

Perform the exercise after or as part of a warm-up, either in a fitness room or on the practice field. Stand on one leg, keeping the knee soft (slightly bent). Raise the opposite leg by bending the knee and hip to 90 degrees. Take the squat to the lowest possible position without losing balance. Pause slightly at the bottom, and then extend back up to the starting position.

Beginning level: Squat and hold for 5 to 10 seconds. Add a side reach with the free leg and rotate a quarter turn to the outside with the free leg to develop all planes of motion (front, photo *a*; side, photo *b*; and rotational, photo *c*).

Single-leg squat, beginning level: *(a)* standard squat, *(b)* with side reach, and *(c)* with rotation.

Advanced level: Hop barefooted onto one foot. As the foot hits the ground, close one eye while lowering into the basic single-leg squat position. Hold the position for 5 seconds.

Soccer specific: Have a teammate toss a soccer ball to you while you dynamically move through the squat, and juggle or pass the ball back and forth.

Dynamic Balance Jumps and Hops

Jumping consists of a takeoff and landing with both feet; hopping involves taking off with one leg and landing on the same leg. Stick the landing and maintain control. You can vary the direction of the jump or hop (forward, sideways, backward, or turning). Progress the exercise only when you can demonstrate a quality landing, absorbing with the whole body.

Beginning level: Jump off from and land with both feet onto a foam mat. Be ready to absorb the landing. Reset yourself on the floor and repeat.

Advanced level: Perform minihurdle (12 in., or 30 cm) lateral hops with a single-leg landing. Use a series of three or four hurdles, set 2 feet (60 cm) apart. Begin by jumping over the hurdles with both feet. After clearing the last hurdle, land on the ground using either your inside foot (the foot closest to the hurdle) or your outside foot (the foot farthest from the last hurdle). Hold the single-leg landing for 2 seconds.

Soccer specific: Perform the same drill as the advanced level and add a ball pass after sticking each single-leg landing. Use an inside or outside foot pass technique. Repeat on the opposite side.

Explosive Bound With Static Hold

Bounds consist of jumping up and out as far as possible. They can be performed by taking off from and landing on the same leg or moving from one leg to the other. Use an explosive takeoff and bound up and out from one leg to the opposite leg, sticking the landing. Try to hold your body in the air as long as possible.

Beginning level: Perform side-to-side bounds with a hold. Jump out sideways from one leg to the opposite leg. Sit into the landing to load the leg without touching the opposite foot to the ground and drive back to the opposite side. Stick the landing and hold for 2 seconds.

Advanced level: Bound diagonally upfield for 10 repetitions. Stick each landing and hold without touching the opposite foot to the ground. Repeat the drill moving backward to increase the difficulty.

Soccer specific: Take a long lateral bound into a vertical jump to head a tossed ball *(a)*. As soon as you land, explode vertically off both feet, tracking the incoming ball for heading *(b)*. Off the header, land on one leg and hold for 1 second; then turn opposite of your landing direction and sprint 10 yards to complete the drill. Repeat to the opposite side.

Explosive bound with static hold, soccer specific.

By incorporating balance training into your program, you can begin to play with greater control. Simple things such as sprinting, cutting to change direction, and striking the ball become sharper and more efficient when you have more control and balance. Make these drills part of your everyday routine for performance improvement as well as injury prevention.

Chapter 5

Total-Body Strength

Transferring acquired strength to competitive situations should be the goal of every athlete. For soccer players, building total-body strength should also be the underlying element of all aspects of physical training. As stated before, a strength foundation can provide the stability and support needed to maintain body postures during movement. It can also springboard improvements in agility, quickness, and speed. General strength improvements will help you to apply and absorb more force when displaying dynamic power in kicking, jumping, and throwing during the match. Strength work should be addressed, at some level, during all phases of training, even during the competition period.

Young players are often misinformed about strength development. Until recently, soccer coaches have not valued strength training. For this reason, most young soccer players have had minimal exposure to a consistent strength program. Some even believe that strength training will make them big, bulky, and slow. By using the appropriate stimulus, this is far from the truth. An effective training program can improve strength for soccer.

STRENGTH TRAINING PRINCIPLES

Before learning how to create actual programs, it is important to understand the basic strength training principles. When you start a new training program, your body interprets the training as stress, something that is considered out of the ordinary. Many athletes believe that they are getting stronger as they perform each repetition. They fail to realize that the actual adaptation and growth occurs after the training session and before the next one. This stress stimulates the body to adapt and become stronger. To use strength training in a positive manner, you need to understand the training principles. These principles include overload, progression, and specificity.

Overload

Simply stated, *overload* means that you do more than you are accustomed to doing. The idea is to stress the body just enough to stimulate positive results. There are a few ways to overload the body during training. The first is to change the intensity, or how hard you work. This refers to the resistance, or weight, used for each exercise. As your muscles and body become comfortable with the workload, you need to increase the intensity to receive more adaptation; otherwise, the body will remain unchanged. For example, you may find push-ups hard to do at the onset of a strength program, but gradually they will be easier as the training cycle progresses. If you continue to use only your body weight and the same number of repetitions, you will most likely not increase your strength level past the initial gains. To improve, you must change the load by adding more resistance (weight vest, weight resting on the back) to shock your body into a new level.

Another way to overload is to change the volume, or the number of repetitions, sets, and exercises. Typically, volume changes as intensity changes. To be effective, you can't raise both at the same time. Early in your training cycle, the volume should be high and the intensity should be low so you can develop your work capacity. As you become accustomed to the amount of work, you can raise the intensity (amount of weight) and reduce the volume (repetitions and sets).

Lastly, changes in overload can be adjusted through the training frequency, or how often you train during a certain period of the year. This pertains to the number of training days a week. Various training rhythms can be applied. If you are training the total body three times a week, you would most likely use the 48-hour rule and train every other day. A split plan would divide the body into upper and lower areas and use a two-days-on and two-days-off approach with two upper-body days and two lower-body days. A maintenance routine would most likely occur twice a week (in-season).

You will need to answer the questions of how much, how many, and how often to fit your individual needs. If the volume or intensity is too high too soon, the chances of overtraining or injury increase. Likewise, if the load is too small or not enough, the training response will be void. This brings us to the principle of progression.

Progression

To avoid overstressing your body, you should have a plan for progressing your strength training program. Start out with moderate workloads that you can handle and then progress in small increments as you improve. You should initially be able to handle the number of repetitions for each set. The resistances will take a backseat to completing the repetitions. Another way to progress your program is to assign intensity levels to each workout. Label the workout as light, moderate, or heavy according to the intensity level. For example, intensity would be low on a light training day (50 to 65 percent of your maximum weight for specific exercises—see page 61 to determine your maximum weight), whereas a heavy training day would warrant intensities above 90 percent. You must also consider where you are in your season because this will affect your energy level; in-season strength training programs should be reduced in volume.

Specificity

Strength training should also be specific to your training needs as well as your sport and even position. For soccer, and most of athletics, strength should be trained as functionally as possible. Vern Gambetta says it best when he refers to "training movements, not muscles." Bodybuilding and powerlifting have lifts and training methods that are specific to the sport of the lifter.

Strength exercises should be multijoint and ground based, while linking the upper and lower body in coordinated movement patterns. Highlighted areas should be the core, the hips, the legs, and the upper body for muscle balance.

TYPES OF STRENGTH

Strength can be developed in many forms. The design of your training program should reflect the strength demands of soccer, which involves dynamic, explosive movements. Such movements require a program whose goal is not necessarily to improve maximal strength or increase size. This is not to say that most young soccer players can't use extra lean muscle to combat the everyday stresses of practice and competition, but more important is the ability to transfer the strength to skills on the field. Table 5.1 lists the types of strength as well as where they fit in the overall scheme of the program. Each category includes the degree of intensity—

Table 5.1   Types of Strength and Their Training Details

Strength category	Intensity	Speed of execution	Application	% of repetition maximum (1RM)	Reps and sets
General strength	Moderate to heavy	Controlled	Overall strength	75-85%	6-8, 3-4
Maximal strength	Heavy to maximal	Slow	Maximal strength	80-100%	1-3, 3-4
Power	Moderate to heavy	Very fast	Explosive power	85-100%	1-5, 4-8
Strength endurance	Light to moderate	Continuous	Work capacity	50-70%	12-25, 2-3

both perceived and as a percentage range of maximum repetition. It also lists the speed of movement as well as the repetition and set range. These parameters will give you a framework so you can get positive results from your strength training program.

General Strength

General strength building refers to building total-body strength in a controlled environment in which the rate of movement is not a concern. Most soccer athletes should spend their time developing general strength using traditional methods. A basic progression with moderate resistance (75 percent of 1RM) working up to heavier training loads (85 percent of 1RM) is used to maximize overall gains. 1RM (1 repetition maximum) is the maximal amount of weight you are able to lift once. See page 61 for how to determine your 1RM.

Maximal Strength

Maximal strength programs are geared toward moving the greatest amount of resistance with no time restriction. This is mainly the focus for powerlifters and competitive weightlifters. Developing this kind of strength demands heavy training loads (up to and even more than 100 percent of 1RM) and low volume. The typical "maxing out" will incorporate this type of effort to perform. This type of training should only be used by experienced athletes because of the potential for injury if performed incorrectly. In my opinion, for most sports, including soccer, this type of strength is not detrimental to performance improvement, but it is unnecessary.

Power

Power, or a combination of strength and speed, is the type of strength most needed by athletes, including soccer players. This is the type of strength that transfers well to the competitive playing area. The focus in training is to move the resistance as fast as possible. The explosive training effect can also be developed through jump training (plyometrics). Understand that you can maximize power training only by developing your general overall strength first. Lacking foundational strength will diminish the effect of power training. This is why this type of strength is developed in a second or third phase of training. Power training is addressed in chapter 6.

Strength Endurance

Strength endurance refers to the ability to repeat muscle contractions over a long period of time. Typically, endurance-based strength programs are used to build work capacity early in most training cycles or after a long layoff from training. As mentioned before, in high-volume workouts, the intensity, or load, is low. Percentages for this type of work are usually between 50 and 70 percent of 1RM, or 10 and 20 percent of body weight.

For soccer players, strength endurance training can be part of early strength sessions as well as the core of training for the competitive phase.

STRENGTH TRAINING METHODS

For the game of soccer, certain strength training methods are more appropriate than others. Remember, strength must transfer to movements on the field. To accomplish this goal, I like to incorporate several training methods to increase strength levels: functional training, circuit training, and power training.

Functional Training

The functional training method uses the basic overload principle and traditional exercises with an emphasis on balance, coordination, and stability while linking muscles to movements. Most of the exercises demand multiple joints, are multidirectional (front, side, diagonal, and rotational), and use the whole body together. For example, performing a dumbbell lunge with an overhead press on the way back up to the starting position develops both lower- and upper-body strength, core strength, balance, and coordination of the muscles involved.

Following are some key points to consider when using functional strength training:

- Use body-weight exercises before adding extra resistance. This will help you to incorporate balance, stability, and coordination in your training while learning proper execution. Too much initial resistance will create inefficient movement patterns.

- Develop core and leg strength first. Core strength will form a foundation to build out to the extremities. The legs and hips will become the stable root system from which to move the rest of the body.

- Athletic movements are coordinated relay systems of primary, antagonistic, and support muscles working together; they are not the result of firing one muscle at a time. Primary muscle refers to the targeted muscle(s) of a particular exercise (biceps in the arm curl). Antagonist muscle refers to the muscle(s) working in opposition to the primary muscle (triceps in the arm curl), whereas supporting muscle lends stability to both muscle groups (shoulder and latissimus in the arm curl). Think linking, not isolating. Envision yourself approaching a flighted ball and getting ready to head it toward the goal. Jumping involves exploding through the ground, using the hip and leg muscles to get in the air. As you elevate, force is transferred through core muscles up through your upper torso to get your body to lean back enough to snap forward and contact the ball as your neck and shoulders isometrically (without shortening or lengthening the muscles) contract.

Circuit Training

The circuit training method involves performing a group of exercises in sequence that are mainly used to develop strength endurance. Circuits can be small (3 or 4 exercises) or large (10 to 12 exercises) and are designed, depending on the desired goal, to be repetition based or time based. Repetition circuits prescribe a certain number of repetitions for every exercise. Once the number of repetitions is completed, the next exercise is performed. During time-based work, a predetermined period of time is set and you complete as many correct repetitions as possible for that allotted time. Circuit training is advantageous if you have limited time to train. I like to use circuit training to reintroduce athletes to training early in the training cycle and during the constraints of in-season schedules when training time is limited.

Following are a few samples of circuits I like to use for developing strength endurance:

Soccer Lower-Body Circuit Workout

1. Dumbbell squat to calf raise × 15 reps
2. 30-second stationary bike sprint or 100-meter sprint
3. Dumbbell side lunge × 12 reps with each leg
4. Physioball supine leg curl × 15 reps
5. 1-minute stationary bike sprint

Complete 3 or 4 sets of this sequence with 1 minute of rest between sets.

Soccer Upper-Body Circuit Workout

1. Dumbbell curl and press × 12 reps
2. Incline body row × 12 reps
3. Upper-body step-up × 12 reps with each arm
4. Seated cable pull-down (pull to the front) × 12 reps
5. Incline push-up × 12 reps

Complete 3 or 4 sets with 1 minute of rest between sets.

Total-Body Circuit (Repetition Based)

1. Dumbbell hang clean × 5 reps
2. Dumbbell squat to an overhead press × 5 reps
3. Dumbbell forward lunge and curl × 5 reps with each leg
4. Dumbbell split jerk × 5 reps
5. Dumbbell squat jump × 5 reps

Complete 5 sets of this sequence with no rest between exercises and 1 minute of rest between sets.

Core Training Circuit (Time Based)

1. Physioball crunch
2. Back extension
3. Seated medicine ball twist
4. V-up
5. Medicine ball standing full circles

Perform each exercise for 30 seconds continuously for 2 or 3 sets.

The following leg circuits are a great way to develop functional strength and build balance, coordination, and work capacity in the lower body. The basic sequence is the idea of Vern Gambetta, expert athletic conditioning coach. Once you've established basic strength and tempo (the goal is 1 rep per second), you can experiment with variations to keep the circuit fresh and the players guessing as to what's in store for the next workout.

Basic Leg Circuit*

1. Body-weight squat to a heel raise × 20 reps
2. Body-weight forward lunge × 20 reps
3. Body-weight step-up (12 in., or 30 cm, step) × 20 reps
4. Squat jump × 10 reps

Perform 2 or 3 sets with 1-minute rests between sets.

Lateral (Side) Emphasized Leg Circuit

1. Body-weight wide-stance squat (lean from one side to the other) × 20 reps
2. Body-weight side lunge × 20 reps
3. Body-weight side step-up × 20 reps
4. Lateral bounds (ice skaters—see chapter 6) × 10 reps

Perform 2 or 3 sets with 1-minute rests between sets.

Basic Half Leg Circuit*

Use this during the season or as a finisher to a strength workout.

1. Body-weight squat × 10 reps
2. Body-weight forward lunge × 10 reps
3. Body-weight step-up × 10 reps
4. Squat jump × 5 reps

Perform 3 or 4 sets with 30 seconds of rest between sets.

*Adapted, by permission, from V. Gambetta, 2007, *Athletic development: The art & science of functional sports conditioning* (Champaign, IL: Human Kinetics), 185-188.

Power Training

Power, or speed strength, is something you'll notice during a soccer performance. Soccer is a game of fast, explosive movements that is very reactive, demanding a demonstration of power. Power training is sometimes referred to as jump training because of the extensive use of plyometric exercises (jumps, hops, and bounds) that involve jumping mechanics. However, power training can be more than jumping. Using exercises that incorporate moderate to heavy resistance with accelerated movement, you'll be able to train your body to display high-speed movements. Medicine ball throws, dumbbell power lifts, and jump training are all great ways to increase athletic power. Once you've developed a basic strength foundation, power training can transfer this strength to your performance. The volume of this type of workout should stay toward the lower end. These exercises are very demanding on the neuromuscular system, and, performed with high-quality execution, a little can go a long way. This is a good method to use during the off-season and near the peak of the preseason. As mentioned, chapter 6 discusses details of power training.

STRENGTH PROGRAM DESIGN GUIDELINES

Use the following suggestions when developing your strength program.

• **How many exercises?** This should be based on the needs of the sport, your training age, and your current training cycle. Strength is important to a soccer player, but not as much as it is to a wrestler or rugby player. About 5 or 6 exercises is usually plenty for the demands of soccer. If your training age is young, you may need to include more exercises to help develop the whole body. During the early phases of training you may want to do between 9 and 12 exercises to help prep your body for more work, but as training continues, this number can drop because of the increased intensity.

• **Which exercises?** Select exercises that involve the whole body and involve a large degree of movement. As mentioned, exercises that develop the hips and legs, the core muscles, and general upper-body areas will produce positive results on the field.

• **How many repetitions and sets?** Do 10 to 15 repetitions to develop strength in the early phases of training. As training progresses and intensity increases, drop the repetitions to between 6 and 8. The number of sets per exercise should stay at 2 or 4 throughout the training phases.

• **What kind of training loads?** Training loads should also progress from light (50 to 60 percent of 1RM) to heavier (85 to 95 percent of 1RM) as the training volume decreases.

• **What about female athletes?** Female athletes need to maintain longer periods of strength building compared to their male counterparts because they normally have limited upper-body strength, physiologically lack the hormone levels to develop muscle, and typically show differences in the distribution of their body composition. These limitations put them at risk for injuries. Knee ligament injuries (namely, ACL) are the most common for female soccer players. Exercise selection should include leg work that involves rotational movement that mimics match play.

DETERMINING STARTING WEIGHTS

Using the correct training intensity is important to gaining strength as well as eliminating unnecessary burnout. You can calculate your training intensities by first evaluating your current strength level. Decide which exercises you want to incorporate into your program. From your list, establish a predicted maximum weight by experimenting with a set or two for each exercise. Perform the exercise for a range of 5 to 10 repetitions. Depending on the number of repetitions you complete, progress the weight until you can perform only a few repetitions. Record the weight and the number of repetitions you complete. For example, when performing a squat, you reach a weight of 180 pounds (82 kg) for 5 repetitions. Use the table in the appendix (pages 185-188) to find your predicted maximum weight (1 repetition maximum, or 1RM). An estimated maximum weight for the exercise used in the example would be around 200 pounds (91 kg) (based on the conversion). You can also perform this procedure on the major exercises and then estimate weight for the secondary movements (a squat versus a biceps curl) using the table. Once you come up with a converted maximum, use that weight to select your training percentages. Depending on the training period, the training percentages would vary from 50 percent of 1RM (for early training periods) to 85 percent of 1RM (for later in the training cycle).

Another way to find your starting weights would be to actually perform test sets, increasing the weight each set until you reach a true 1 repetition maximum weight. This is fine for the experienced lifter but could be dangerous for the inexperienced athlete. It is not the method to use if you've been away from training for multiple weeks and are just starting back up.

These methods have been traditionally used for identifying starting weights for the major exercises. But what about the secondary exercises? For auxiliary exercises such as a dumbbell curl and press or a triceps push-down, the need for exact starting resistance is not as crucial. Select a resistance that is challenging but gives you the ability to complete the exercise set.

STRENGTH EXERCISES

The following section describes strength exercises that are classified as follows: squatting movements, lunging, stepping movements, single-leg exercises, pushing exercises, pulling exercises, and core exercises. Most strength exercises fall into one of these categories. Each exercise description explains the movement, the equipment involved, and the focal point.

SQUATTING MOVEMENTS

The focus of squatting movement exercises is to strengthen the leg muscles (quadriceps, hamstrings, gluteals, and ankle muscles).

Barbell Squat

Use a power rack or bar standards to place a barbell at chest height. Walk under the bar to place it on your upper-back muscles. Lift the bar off the rack and back up a step to clear the standards. Stand with your feet parallel and just outside shoulder width. Lower your body under control to a position just below parallel while keeping your torso erect. Move explosively back to the starting position by extending the ankle, knee, and hip.

Front Squat

With the same setup as the back squat, position the bar across the front part of your shoulders with your hands facing upward and your elbows raised as high as possible. Execute the squat while maintaining a tight posture and attaining the same depth as the back squat.

Dumbbell Squat

Hold a pair of dumbbells down by your sides. Perform the squat. Add an overhead press at the finish of the squat to incorporate total-body movement.

Body-Weight Squat

This exercise can be performed with your hands overhead or at your waist. Stand with your feet about shoulder-width apart. Bend at the knees and squat as low as possible with control. Accelerate from the bottom position back to the start. The tempo is 1 repetition every second.

LUNGES

Lunge exercises develop the leg muscles, primarily the hamstrings and gluteals.

Forward Lunge

Hold two dumbbells down at your sides. Step one foot about 2 or 3 feet out (60 to 90 cm) to the front, bend your knees, and lower your hips toward the ground. Don't let your back knee touch the floor. Keep the lead knee over the front foot but not farther. Be explosive and drive off the lead leg to get back to the starting position.

Lateral Lunge

Hold dumbbells by your sides. Take a long step to the side and shift your weight to your lead foot by sitting down through your hips. Keep both feet flat and your chest up as you lower your body. The trail leg is straight. Push off the ground with the lead leg and return to the starting position. Repeat to the opposite side.

Backward Lunge

Hold dumbbells by your sides. Take a long step back and lower your hips toward the ground, keeping your front knee over your front foot *(a)*. The front heel is flat and the back heel is off the ground *(b)*. Bring the back leg to the front to return to the starting position. Repeat with the opposite leg.

Rotational Lunge

Hold dumbbells at your sides. Take a step backward on a 45-degree angle to the right or left *(a)*. Rotate your whole body as your foot strikes the ground, and lower your hips toward the floor *(b)*. Return to the starting position by rotating back to the original position. The lead knee will be over the foot. Repeat using the opposite leg.

STEPPING EXERCISES

Stepping exercises focus on developing the hamstrings and gluteals.

Forward Step-Up

Use a stable step with various heights (12, 18, or 21 in., or 30, 45, or 53 cm). Hold dumbbells at your sides. Stand facing the step. Step one leg up onto the step, followed by the other leg. Step down and repeat. You can use one leg at a time or alternate.

Side Step-Up

Stand sideways to a step and hold dumbbells at your sides. Step up with the leg closest to the step. Follow with the other leg; then step down and repeat.

Rotational Step-Up

Hold dumbbells at your sides and stand to the side of a step *(a)*. The step should be at a 45-degree angle behind you to your left or right. Step up on the backward angle *(b)*. Follow with the other leg; then step down and repeat.

SINGLE-LEG EXERCISES

The following exercises develop unilateral (single) leg strength in the quadriceps, gluteals, and hamstrings, and also develop balance.

Supported Single-Leg Squat

Stand a few steps in front of a supporting box, step, or bench. Prop one leg on the support step behind you. Bring the working leg out in front of you at about the length you would when performing a lunge, keeping your knee over your foot. Lower your hips down toward the floor as far as possible and then back to the starting point.

Split Squat

Open your legs to a wide split position with one leg forward and the other back. Hold dumbbells at your sides or use a barbell in the back squat position (a). Keeping your torso in an upright position, lower yourself down to the floor without your back knee touching (b). Raise back up, keeping your legs in the split position. Perform all the repetitions for one leg; then switch legs.

Single-Leg Romanian Deadlift

Holding dumbbells at your sides, stand on one leg while keeping your torso flat as you lower the weights toward the ground. The off leg will swing behind to counterbalance your forward movement. Keeping the balancing leg slightly bent to keep from hyperextending, reach down as far as possible without losing your position. Repeat the exercise on the opposite leg.

Medicine Ball Single-Leg Hip Bridge

Lying on the floor supine (on your back), place one foot on a medicine ball with your knee bent. The opposite leg will remain straight throughout the exercise and will be raised off the floor to the point where it is level with the opposite knee. Contract your core muscles and lift your hips off the floor. Hold the elevated position for 2 seconds, and then relax back to the starting position. Repeat the exercise with the opposite leg.

Physioball Leg Curl

Using an air-filled physioball (also called a stability ball), lie on your back and rest both feet on the ball. Contract your core muscles and raise your hips off the floor *(a)*. Bend your legs and pull both feet in toward your body while keeping your hips off the floor *(b)*. Pause for 2 counts; then slowly bring your legs back out to the starting point and your hips to the ground.

PUSHING EXERCISES

Pushing exercises develop strength in the front upper torso (chest, triceps, and shoulders).

Bench Chest Press

Using a flat bench with bar standards, assume a supine position on the bench. Take the bar in an overhand grip with your hands just outside shoulder width, arms extended over your chest. Under control, lower the bar down to the middle of your chest *(a)*. Touch your chest and explode back to the starting position, keeping your head and shoulders in contact with the bench and your feet on the floor *(b)*. Inclining the bench can be used as a variation.

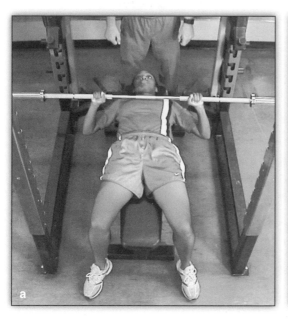 

Dumbbell Single-Arm Chest Press

Hold a dumbbell in one hand and position yourself faceup on a utility bench. Perform a normal pressing movement while activating your core muscles on the opposite side. Repeat the exercise with the opposite arm.

Standing Band Press

Use a medium to heavy exercise band attached to a rack or other fixed apparatus at about shoulder height. Stand facing away from the attached end with your feet in a staggered position (one foot in front of the other; photo *a*). Press the band with both or alternating arms to a fully extended position *(b)*.

Standing Dumbbell Rotating Shoulder Press

Start the movement in a standing position with a pair of dumbbells at shoulder height *(a)*. Your palms should be facing each other. Rotating your torso to one side, raise the weight with either both or alternating arms in a rotational pattern (palms facing in at the start to palms facing forward at the end; photo *b*).

Push-Up Series

Perform standard push-ups using various hand positions as well as adding unstable situations. I like to use the following variations for variety and a challenge:

- *Incline push-up.* This position targets the upper chest and shoulders along with the triceps. Place your hands on a box, bench, or rack to raise them higher than your feet *(a-b)*.
- *Decline push-up.* This position targets the lower chest and triceps. Place your feet on a box, bench, or rack to raise them higher than your hands *(c)*.
- *Medicine ball (double or single arms) push-up.* This variation challenges the stabilizers of the core as well as the major upper-body musculature. In a push-up position, place your hands on top of a medicine ball *(d)*. Perform the push-up while maintaining control on the ball. Repeat putting your feet on the ball instead *(e)*.

Push-up series: *(a-b)* incline push-up, *(c)* decline push-up, *(d)* medicine ball push-up with hands on ball, and *(e)* medicine ball push-up with feet on ball.

Upper-Body Step-Up

This exercise targets the upper body and the core musculature and helps with balance and stability in the upper extremities.

Using a 6- to 12-inch (15 to 30 cm) box or step, hand walk up and over the step from a push-up position. Activate your core muscles to help you stabilize during the movement. Try the following variations:

- *Forward, up and down.* With the step in front of you, hand walk up and down.
- *Lateral, up and down.* With the step to the side of your position, hand walk sideways over the step and to the other side *(a-c)*. Repeat in the opposite direction.
- *Crossover from one side to the other.* With the step to the side, lead the arm step-up with the hand that is farthest from the step (a crossover pattern). Bring the other hand to the floor on the opposite side first. Repeat to the other side.

PULLING EXERCISES

Pulling exercises strengthen the upper rear torso muscles and arms—specifically, the latissimus dorsi, biceps, rear shoulder, and mid-back.

Seated Pull-Down

Use a cable weight stack. Sit in the seat and grab a bar using a shoulder-width overhand grip, with arms overhead (a). Set your torso slightly back and begin to pull the bar down to your chest. Slowly return the bar back to the starting point (b). Vary the grip by turning your hands to an underhand position (c).

Seated pull-down: (a) start and (b) finish; (c) reverse grip.

Body Row ⊙ DVD

Set a bar in a power rack about 3 feet (90 cm) from the floor. Position yourself on your back under the bar (your eyes should be even with the bar). Grab the bar with an overhand grip and place your body off the floor while maintaining a tight posture (straight line). Begin pulling yourself up toward the bar, simulating a pull-up. Lower yourself under control back to the starting position without your body touching the ground.

Dumbbell Row

Place one knee and the same-side hand on a bench. The other foot is on the ground to maintain balance, while the other hand is holding a dumbbell down toward the floor *(a)*. Pull the weight up to the side of your body with your elbow high *(b)*. Lower the weight back down to a full stretch position. Repeat the exercise to the opposite arm.

DUMBBELL SHOULDER COMBINATIONS

These exercises strengthen all three areas of the shoulders (anterior, middle, and posterior deltoids), the upper back, and the arms.

Front Raise

Stand and hold a dumbbell in each hand. Start the exercise with the weights resting on your thighs and your palms down. Keeping your arms straight, raise the weights up to shoulder height, stopping when your arms are parallel to the floor.

Side Raise

Stand and hold a dumbbell in each hand. Start with the weights at your sides and your palms facing your legs. Keeping your arms straight, raise the dumbbells straight out to the sides until your arms are parallel to the floor.

Upright Row

Stand holding dumbbells down in front of you, with your palms facing your legs *(a)*. Raise the weights up to chin level by bending your arms with your elbows out to the sides *(b)*. Lower the weight back to the starting position with control.

Rear Shoulder Raise

Bend at the waist so that your upper torso is leaning forward. Keep your back flat and your chest out. Hold the dumbbells with your arms hanging down straight *(a)*. Raise the dumbbells out to your sides, keeping your arms straight *(b)*. Lower the weights under control back to the starting position.

Dumbbell Curl and Press

Hold dumbbells down by your sides with your palms facing front. Curl the weights up by bending your arms at the elbows so the weights reach shoulder level *(a)*. At this point, rotate your palms inward (facing each other) and press the weights over your head, while rotating the palms away from your body, to a locked-out position *(b)*. Retrace the movement back to the starting point.

CORE TRAINING

In today's fitness world, the big buzzwords are *core* and *core training*. These terms mean different things to different athletes. Athletes tend to think that training the core means working the abdominal muscles exclusively. Although "abs" are core muscles, they are only a part of the big picture. When training core strength, you should think of the body as a whole. Doing only multiple crunches would not benefit your performance.

The core structure is composed of all the muscles, both big and small, that connect and cross the center of the body. This includes the muscles in the back and hips. They form the structure and foundation for initiating and decelerating motion and affect everything you do as a player, from sprinting to kicking to throw-ins. To develop the core for athletics, you must perform some exercises on your feet if you hope to transfer the gains to the game. Examples of core exercises performed on the feet include the medicine ball diagonal chop and the medicine ball single-leg box pattern. Training must also be as dynamic as possible. It's OK to start out with structural work by slowing down the movement and concentrating on the target—in other words, isolating muscles or muscle groups. However, this is not the environment in which you will be performing. On the field everything is fast, furious, and reactive. Because you have to be able to produce and reduce all types of force on the field, this is what you should focus on in your core training program. By developing the strength and stability in core muscles, you'll be able to transfer it to the power exercises and drills in chapter 6, and eventually to the field.

CORE EXERCISES

The core exercises described in this section are grouped by how they are performed: seated, stationary, or standing using a medicine ball; and as rotations, twists, and chops. Perform 2 or 3 sets and 10 to 20 repetitions for each exercise. Be progressive in the volume, and remember to reduce the number of repetitions if you increase the volume (through added resistance).

SEATED, STATIONARY, OR USING APPARATUS

Back Extension

On a glute-hamstring raise apparatus, get in a prone position with your feet secured in the footrest. Lower your upper body, with your hands behind your head, by bending at the waist to the lowest possible position *(a)*. Extend back up to a position parallel to the floor and pause for 2 counts *(b)*. You can incorporate a rotation by turning to the right or left on the way up.

 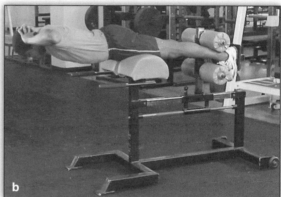

Seated Medicine Ball Twist

Sit on the ground and hold a medicine ball at waist height with your feet off the ground about 6 inches (15 cm) and your legs slightly bent. Begin twisting back and forth, turning your shoulders perpendicular to the rest of your body. The action should be dynamic with control.

Hanging Knee Raise

Hang from an overhead rack or bar by using a pull-up grip with your hands, or use an arm cuff attached to the bar. Start by pulling your knees to your chest and pause at the top *(a)*. Lower your legs under control back to the starting point. A variation to the basic move is to rotate your knees to the right or left *(b)*.

Hanging knee raise: *(a)* standard and *(b)* twisting variation.

Bench Rotating Sit-Up

Lie on one side on a bench with your hips slightly bent and off the edge. Position your hands behind your head. Have a partner hold your lower legs down by sitting on them without applying too much pressure *(a)*. Start the move by flexing at the waist and rotating so that you are facing your partner at the top of the movement *(b)*.

Body Bridge

This a standard core strengthening exercise also known as a body plank or human arrow. Position yourself on the ground in a prone position. Bend your elbows and tuck them at your sides, and keep your legs straight. Begin by contracting your core muscles; then raise your hips off the ground so that your body is in a straight line, resting on your elbows and toes (see figure 2.8 on page 23). You can also vary this by using a side *(a-b)* or supine (back facing the ground; photo *c*) position.

Body bridge. *(a)* side bridge, *(b)* side bridge with arm raise, *(c)* back bridge.

V-Up

Lying faceup on the floor, position your arms over your head with your legs fully extended on the floor *(a)*. Begin by simultaneously bringing your arms and legs together by bending at the waist. Contract through the midsection of your body so that your shoulders come off the ground as high as possible *(b)*. Pause at the top and then lower back to the floor under control.

ROTATIONS, TWISTS, AND CHOPS

All of the twists, chops, and rotations can be performed while walking or lunging to increase the intensity.

Standing Medicine Ball Twist

Holding a medicine ball at chest height, twist back and forth by working through the body midsection. Rotate enough so that your back foot pivots with your heel off the ground. Progress with more speed as you gain confidence with the movement.

Medicine Ball Vertical Chop

Hold the medicine ball overhead in both hands with your feet wide apart *(a)*. Move the ball down toward the ground in a chopping pattern by flexing at the waist *(b)*. Extend back up to the starting point.

Medicine Ball Diagonal Chop

Stand with your feet apart and hold a medicine ball in both hands. Start the ball above your head on the right *(a)*. Chop the ball down and across your body to the opposite ankle by flexing at the waist *(b)*. Repeat the exercise on the opposite side.

Medicine Ball Full Circle Rotation

Hold the ball above your head with your arms extended. Bring the ball down and around in a circular pattern, working through your waist. The ball should be about 2 inches (5 cm) off the ground at the bottom of the movement. Repeat the exercise in the opposite direction.

Medicine Ball Single-Leg Figure Eight

Stand and balance on one leg, holding the medicine ball at chest height. Begin by moving the ball in a standing figure eight pattern while you maintain balance. Reverse the direction on the ball. Change to the opposite foot.

Medicine Ball Single-Leg Box Pattern

While balancing on one foot, take the medicine ball through a square pattern, holding the ball out in front of your body. The bottom of the square should take you down as low as possible.

Chapter 6 describes how your strength can be converted into explosive power that becomes a premium on the field. Strength gains developed through training will pay huge dividends in all aspects of your performance. Use circuit training during early training periods as well as in-season situations to build work volume and to make use of limited time during the competitive season. Build total-body strength and power in the off-season training phase to improve your performance. All of your strength training phases should have a functional approach with core training as the focal point. Follow a progressive plan that maintains consistency and attacks your specific training goals.

Chapter 6

Explosive Power

P ower development is a key component of soccer performance. Think about the many times on the field that you are called on to be reactive and explosive in your effort—driving a crossing pass, vertical jumping into a header at the goal, or exploding to meet the ball at its highest point as the keeper. To be effective, power training should follow the foundational strength phase of the training program. As mentioned before, foundational strength is critical for all aspects of physical training, including power development. Without foundational strength, power is limited.

In basic terms, power is strength and speed combined. It involves moving a resistance without hesitation, whether it's a dumbbell, a medicine ball, or your body. This type of training is very demanding in terms of neuro-muscular involvement. If you train with the right intensity, your body will feel taxed. This is why power training should not be scheduled for every workout unless it involves minimum volume with emphasis on different aspects (jumping one day and throwing the next).

Power-type training was initially used for training track and field athletes. This is why the majority of the drills involve jumping, heaving, or throw-ing. The term *plyometrics* is also associated with these drills. Plyometrics take the muscle's natural response to stretch to increase an opposing reaction (force production). Think of a muscle as a rubber band. The more tension and stretch you put on the band, the more quickly the band will snap back with added force. This concept can be applied to many muscle groups, both in the upper and lower body. Recently, most athletes, including soccer players, have undertaken plyometric work through jump training. However, power training can be more than just jumping. We'll examine total-body medicine ball throws that can help to peak your power along with power-developing lifts (power pulls, cleans, presses, and jerks).

As your strength improves, you will notice that you can control and gener-ate force more efficiently. The key is to understand how to generate the power from the ground up through the core and out through the extremities (arms and legs). Without the proper strength gains, this linkage can get dampened. This is very evident in athletes with a low training age (i.e., limited training experience). An athlete with a low training age can be a chronologically younger or older athlete but with limited training experience. The ability to slow down force and then quickly redirect it will be incomplete and delayed without proper strength levels. Until you have good leg and core stability when jumping or performing basic leg movements, with no buckling over or folding forward, you should keep developing your strength and stick with low-level power drills (small hops or jumps, jumping rope).

Initially, power training should focus on drills and exercises that involve remedial work to increase control and stability when reducing force (eccentric strength). Taking a simple hop or jump in various directions and concentrating on a soft (quiet) landing is a good way to start this process.

POWER CONCEPTS

This section describes various techniques to explain how power is developed for performance improvement. Most of these techniques may seem very elementary, but to produce maximum results, you need to master certain foundational movements. Notice that the landing technique precedes the jumping up technique. This is because the hardest part of jumping up or out is executing a good stable landing. This progression is a good way to evaluate your current strength level. Once it is clear that you can stabilize when landing, the intensity of your power development can literally take off.

Landing

By watching how players strike the ground when sprinting, cutting, or jumping, you can see how a lack of control is a deficit when performing. The ability to stabilize quickly on each step or landing can greatly help reduce the force on the body and give you better power production. Once you leave the ground, the force can be as much as six times your body weight upon return! When working on landing mechanics, I instruct athletes to "land as soft as a feather." They should be able to hold the landing for a few seconds without losing their balance or, for single-leg work, touching the other foot to the ground. The hips, knees, and ankles should be in a loaded position with each joint flexed and the back in a flat posture. This is the opposite of force production posture, in which these joints are extended forcefully. Drills should not progress until the athlete can perform this basic drill.

Jumping Down

The next technique to master after the landing is elevating the intensity of the landing by raising the height and distance that you land from. This is also a lead-up to the most intense plyometric exercise, the depth jump. Vary the height as you progress, but be conscious of only using a height that you can control. Start by just stepping off the height (8 to 10 in., or 20 to 25 cm) to a proper landing. Follow this by actually jumping down and sticking the landing with good posture. Once you have established good control on these drills, perform a set or two as warm-up for high-intensity jump training. The exercise can be done with both double- and single-leg landings.

Jumping Up

Follow your landing drills with jumping to an elevated surface (a box, bench, or step). Like jumping down, this may seem trivial, but the focus is to properly execute the basic extension and landing of the body. I like to use a low height (knee level), medium height (mid-thigh), and high height (waist level) when progressing this technique. Concentrate on the projection of the hips up and out at all jumping levels. This will cause you to fully extend your body and get your center of mass in the right position. When making contact with the landing surface, stick and stabilize as with jumping down.

Loading and Unloading the Arms and Legs

Creating power in the body starts with the center of the body and must finish through the legs and arms (more specifically, the toes and fingers) to create maximum production. I've witnessed great players who have trouble coordinating their arms and legs in a vertical jump test. This limits their power transfer. Using your total body will add quality to power training. The loading aspect should make your body feel like a loaded spring. The arms are flexed and rigid with the elbows behind your back. The hips, knees, and ankles are flexed with the torso tight (figure 6.1a). The unloading posture now becomes the opposite of loading—extension of the ankles, knees, and hips with the arms swinging overhead, up and out (figure 6.1b). This basic concept can now be applied to all explosive movements (hopping, sprinting, cutting, jumping, and throwing).

Figure 6.1   (a) Loading and (b) unloading positions.

Hopping

Hopping refers to taking off on one foot and landing on that same foot. This can be a low-level stability hop or a high-intensity single-leg hurdle hop. Increasing the vertical distance of the hop will increase the stress of the landing. Hopping will give you quick feedback on your single-leg strength level. Single-leg strength is critical to increasing speed and cutting mechanics.

Power Jumping

Jumping involves both vertical and horizontal movements. It implies a two-foot takeoff and landing. Jumping can be as simple as jumping rope or as complex as high-level depth jumps. Once again, raising the vertical demand will increase the stress load. All aspects of loading and unloading your body apply when performing jumps. Because jumping has a heavy neuromuscular demand, a high volume is not necessary to achieve a good training effect; in fact, too much power jumping can be counterproductive to overall training.

Bounding

Bounding is considered an advanced-level plyometric or explosive drill. It demands great hip and length strength to be able to stabilize ground contact and produce repetitive explosive takeoffs. The majority of bounds involve horizontal projection of the body. Most drills will have you take off with one leg and land on the opposite leg as explosively as possible. I like to cue these drills by using the term *hang time* to get the athletes to hold their flight time (stay in the air) as long as possible. Bounds can be applied to all directions of movement.

Explosive Weight Training

Explosive power can also be developed by combining basic strength gains with fast, reactive movements. Typically, the Olympic-style lifts (the clean and jerk and the snatch) have been popular with power-seeking athletes. These lifts are a standard of American football programs, in which the majority of players have a lot of experience with weightlifting. These lifts are very technical and demand a large amount of instruction and attention.

The primary reason for soccer athletes to use explosive weight training is to develop total-body power through triple extension of the ankle, knee, and hip. The actual receiving and stabilizing of the bar overhead or in the "rack" position, which is technically the most demanding part, can be eliminated without losing this training concept. For example, doing a high pull instead of a power clean eliminates the catch phase of the clean but does not affect the triple extension of the body. A high pull incorporates the same pulling action of the ankles, knees, and hips with the legs, but the arms are used simply in a rowing manner. Dumbbells can also be a good alternative to use when performing these lifts, as they allow for more range of motion and adaptability because the athlete is not locked into one plane of motion.

Total-Body Medicine Ball Throws

To truly develop maximum power when using resistance, the resistance should be eventually released. Normally, when using dumbbells or other weight equipment, the speed of executing the movement must slow down at the end to keep the resistance from taking you off the ground. Medicine ball throwing addresses this issue. Using a moderate load, you'll be able to perform a wide range of power throws in which you can release the implement without losing maximum speed. These drills can create a more natural play environment for the soccer athlete, one that is reactive and spontaneous. Doing medicine ball throws with a partner can develop cooperative skills for team transfer. A wall inside or outside can be used when training alone.

POWER PROGRAM DESIGN

To design a consistent and comprehensive power program for soccer, you need to separate the many forms of power training into activities that are appropriate for your needs. Low-intensity drills are a good starting point. Keep in mind that the load (resistance) of power exercises doesn't need to be heavy to get a training effect. In fact, research in power development indicates that loads between 30 and 50 percent of maximum are optimal for peak power training. For most young players, body weight will be sufficient for training. Understand, as stated before, that vertical load is more demanding than horizontal load, and single-leg work is more stressful than double-leg, supported drills. Also, when performing hops and jumps, single-response (one at a time) repetitions are less difficult than multiple-response (without stopping) work. Table 6.1 on page 92 categorizes drills to help you organize your workouts.

In designing your power development program, keep in mind that these drills have a high neuromuscular (stress) component. You should perform them at low volume to ensure that you execute the speed correctly. Performing these drills when you are fatigued will decrease the chance of training at peak force production and transferring that training to the field. Power training should be done early in the training session and prior to any endurance type of training.

Start power training once or twice a week with stability landing repetitions and low-impact hopping or jumping (i.e., rope jumping). Perform 2 or 3 landing-emphasized sets (8 to 10 reps) and 3 sets of low-impact hops or jumps (8 to 10 reps).

Table 6.1 Categories of Power Drills

Category	Purpose	Intensity	Repetition response	Direction of movement
Rope jumping	Ankle–foot reactive response	Low	Single or multiple	Vertical
Stability landings (single or double leg)	Landing technique and control, eccentric strength	Low to moderate	Single or multiple	Vertical or horizontal
Single- and double-leg hopping	Reactive response	Low to moderate	Multiple	Vertical or horizontal
Jumping up: box/hurdle	Explosive power, reactive response	Moderate to high	Single or multiple	Vertical
Jumping down/ depth jumps	Eccentric strength, reactive response	Moderate to high	Single	Vertical
Bounding: multidirectional	Reactive power	High	Multiple	Horizontal
Total-body medicine ball throws	Explosive power	High	Single; multiple when using wall	Horizontal

After 2 weeks, increase the intensity by performing higher or longer jumps (increase 3 to 6 in., or 8 to 15 cm) and introducing medicine ball throws. Use a 2- to 3-kilogram ball (around 4 to 6 lb.) and perform 2 sets of 10 repetitions of various positions.

After this initial phase (4 weeks), jumping drills can increase to maximum height or distance, using 4 or 5 sets of 3 to 5 repetitions. At this point introduce bounding drills and perform to 20-yard distances, attempting to cover as much distance possible on each bound. Do 3 to 5 sets.

There has been much discussion regarding jump training and tracking the number of contacts (jump landings) the athlete performs. The concern is that too many heavy landings can produce unwanted stress. This can be true if the volume is not regulated. If volume stays at a moderate level and recovery days are incorporated, power workouts can be very beneficial. Be more aware of the technique of each drill and the speed of execution. If you feel the speed of the drill slowing down or your technique breaking down, it is probably a good indication that it's time to stop the drill session.

EXPLOSIVE POWER DRILLS

This section offers recommendations for soccer power drills. Most of these drills can be done on the field or in an indoor facility (agility room, gymnasium). Make sure the landing area is clear of debris or unsafe obstacles. The surface should yield to the impact of your body. Your training attire should give you freedom of movement and be nonrestricting, and your shoes should be slip resistant.

Rope Jumping

- *Two-foot jumps.* Turn the rope while jumping with both feet, using mostly the ankle and foot. The rope can be turned both forward and backward. Jump for quickness rather than height.

- *Single-leg jumps.* Use the same technique as for the two-foot jumps but with one foot. Transition the jumps to the opposite foot without stopping.

- *Shuffle jumps.* As you turn the rope, alternate shuffle steps both forward and backward and in and out.

- *High-knee running.* Run in place with your knees up high. This should have a quick tempo.

- *Combos.* Combine several different jumps, steps, and tempos to increase the intensity.

Stability Hops With Landing Emphasis

- *Single-leg stability hops (vertical).* Jump off both feet and land on your right or left foot, sticking the ground softly. Repeat the jump using both legs to take off. Increase the intensity by increasing the jumping height. Hold the landing for 3 to 5 seconds.

- *Single-leg stability hops (horizontal).* Start on one foot and hop out, landing on the same foot. Stick the landing softly. Use multiple directions to move down the floor or field (forward, backward, laterally, and diagonally).

- *Two-foot stability jumps (vertical).* Jump off two feet as high as possible and land as softly as possible. Stick and hold the landing.

- *Two-foot stability jumps (horizontal).* Move down the field by explosively jumping for distance. Hold the landing and stabilize.

Jumps

- *Squat jumps.* Load your hips and legs and quickly extend vertically. Your arms will extend overhead at the height of the jump. Repeat as you land in a quick, reactive response into the next jump. Increase the intensity by taking your arms out of the jump (place them on your hips or behind your head).
- *Tuck jumps.* Jump using the same technique as the squat jump and bring your knees as close as possible to your chest while in the air.

Tuck jump.

Multidirectional Hurdle Jumps

Use hurdles of various heights (12, 18, 21, or 24 in., or 30, 45, 53, or 60 cm) and set them 3 feet (90 cm) apart in a row, alternating between facing forward and facing to the side. Jump over the hurdles while bringing your knees up toward your chest. Land softly and begin the next jump as quickly as possible, eliminating a long ground contact time. Hold each landing in a squat position for 2 to 4 seconds or add a 180-degree or rotational turn to increase the intensity of the drill.

Box Jumps

- *Single response.* Set up a knee-high stable box with a padded surface. Load your body by flexing your ankles, knees, and hips as well as cocking your arms behind your body. Forcefully extend your body to elevate your hips high in the air and project yourself onto the box. Step off the box and reset for the next jump. Variations include side or rotating jumps to the box.
- *Multiple response.* Choosing a box from knee to waist height, explosively jump up and down, concentrating on a quick reactive rhythm. You can also use a row of boxes set at various heights.

Depth Jumps

The depth jump is very demanding because of the increased landing load coming down from a higher surface; it should be considered an advanced jumping technique. Jump off a box, bench, or step that is 24 to 36 inches (60 to 90 cm) high and land softly. Without hesitation, jump over a hurdle and stick and hold the landing. Progress the height only if the previous height becomes less challenging.

Jumping Drills on the Field

- *Header repeats.* Have a teammate or partner toss soccer balls to your head as you meet each ball at its highest point. Think about elevating to maximum height on each jump.
- *Multidirectional ball jumps.* Place a soccer ball on the ground and stand on one side. Begin jumping quickly to the other side, then on a diagonal backward, followed by a forward jump and another backward jump. Repeat this pattern for 10 seconds, and then accelerate for 10 yards.

Bounding Drills ◉ 📀

- *Alternating forward bound.* Using a yielding surface (turf or grass field), build up to a full-speed sprint for about 30 yards. From this point begin the explosive bounds, moving from one foot to the other. Carry this movement for approximately 30 yards and then gradually slow down to stop. Recover (1.5 to 2 min.) before starting the next repetition.

- *Diagonal bound.* Use the same technique as the forward bound except push off to a diagonal direction both right and left.

- *Single-leg forward bound.* Perform a forward bound on one leg. Pull your knee up in an explosive manner, using your arms forcefully. Land softly on the same leg and repeat the next takeoff without hesitation. Try to cover a distance of 15 to 20 yards, and repeat using the opposite leg.

- *Lateral bound (ice skater).* These bounds can be performed in place or by moving sideways repeatedly. Load your body by flexing your ankles, knees, and hips as you land from one side to the other. Throw your arms apart forcefully to get maximum distance. Touch the opposite hand of the leg you're landing on to the ground to keep your center of gravity low.

Medicine Ball Total-Body Throws ◉ 📀

- *Squat and push.* Hold the medicine ball at chest level while squatting to load your body *(a)*. Push the ball out as if throwing a basketball chest pass. Release the ball as far as you can *(b)*. Your momentum will cause you to jump forward off the ground.

- *Squat and scoop.* Hold the ball between your feet and squat down (the ball should be close to the ground; photo *a*). Extend your body forward, finishing with your arms high as you release the ball *(b)*. Your momentum should take you off the ground.

- *Side rotational.* Turn your body to one side and load the ball to the hip of the opposite direction of your throw *(a)*. Rotate your torso and forcefully release the ball across the front of your body, finishing with the arms extended *(b)*. Repeat the throw to the opposite side.

• *Over the back.* Squat down and hold the ball between your knees with extended arms *(a)*. Lean back and, using your legs to generate force, swing your arms up and overhead to release the ball *(b)*. Finish with your arms extended.

• *Single-leg squat and push.* Hold the ball at chest height while squatting on one leg. Extend your body and release the ball, finishing with your arms fully extended.

To increase your power on the field, select drills that are brief, reactive, and explosive. Challenge yourself both horizontally and vertically and through all planes of motion to transfer power to your work on the field. Keep power development as a product of your strength development because a solid strength foundation will ignite your power to higher levels. Chapter 7 discusses speed development, which, along with agility, is a high premium for players on the field.

Chapter **7**

Speed

As we have discovered, strength and power components are of high priority for performance improvement on the soccer field. Speed is just as important. Though the demand for speed varies from one position to the next, it affects a player's performance level tremendously. Game speed can change the outcome of many situations on the field. At North Carolina, we build our playing strategy on our players' speed. For our teams, the focus of speed training is to make them more athletic soccer players.

Is speed inherent? To some extent, it is. However, speed can be taught and improved. This doesn't mean that after a few training sessions you will be dramatically faster, but over time, basic technical drills can give you the chance to reach your speed potential.

Speed training should be carefully balanced with your strength and power work because, if performed correctly, it will stress the nervous system just as much. Performing high-velocity drills for consecutive workouts or days will eventually diminish positive results. This type of training, along with power training, needs to be performed at or near full speed to receive the training effect. Laboring through or practicing slow movements will produce only minimal results. When finishing a speed session, you should feel worked but not totally exhausted. The program design section will give you specific suggestions for planning a successful program.

Soccer-specific speed training requires combinations of acceleration, tempo changes, and multidirectional reacceleration. Many soccer players believe that they must sustain their speed continuously for the entire 90 minutes of the game. In fact, in many high-level games the average time and distance a player sprints on the field is very low (for a keeper it is obviously even less). For this reason, soccer speed training should concentrate on starting and restarting skills as well as rapid change-of-direction drills, which will be addressed in chapter 8, Agility.

To improve top-end speed (how fast you can run), you need to understand and practice the basic mechanics of sprinting, including posture, stride frequency, and stride length. Once you have mastered these basic mechanics, you can apply them to the specific speed needs of soccer—acceleration and top-end speed.

Speed development can also spill over into specific conditioning (speed endurance) training for developing anaerobic capacity specific for the game as well as a particular position. Speed endurance is the ability to perform high-quality sprint intervals over a period of time in a fatigued state. As fatigue sets in, technique tends to get compromised. To play multiple quality minutes, you'll need to be able to sprint efficiently over a period of time.

Acceleration involves getting the body moving to full speed as quickly as possible. It demands adopting a pushing posture to apply force into the ground. This driving mode is what creates explosive pickup when trying to get into position or maneuver past an opponent. A combination of power and strength becomes key when focusing on acceleration. Many soccer players spend endless hours trying to develop speed through what is really speed endurance work (training speed in a fatigued mode and without regard to recovery). They perform semimaximum speed runs that dampen the explosive nature of acceleration and all-out top speed. When working speed-type drills, keep in mind that sessions should contain high-intensity work with enough recovery in between to sustain quality. Also, this type of training should be hard but not to the extent that your body can't recover for the next day's workout.

SPEED PROGRAM DESIGN

When planning your speed development program, allow sufficient recovery between intensive bouts and adjust the volume (how much you work) to lessen the chance of overtraining. Speed training should be just that, speed training, not speed endurance or conditioning. Use a combination of starting, acceleration, and top-speed training exercises to improve the dynamics of your movement in the game.

Following are some speed programming guidelines:

- If you are training multiple components in one session, speed should be trained first or early in the session.
- Choose proper shoes and clothing that won't restrict your movement and that provide good traction.
- Starts and acceleration can be trained more than once a week. Keep the volume low and the intensity high. Remember, training speed under fatigue will break down technique.

- Use a rest-to-work ratio of 3:1 or 4:1 when training speed. For example, if a resisted sprint takes you 10 seconds to complete, you should recover for 30 seconds before starting the next repetition. This will allow you to repeat quality effort on each repetition.

- Choose 2 or 3 drills, 5 to 10 repetitions, and 2 or 3 sets for any of the drills. You don't have to perform a ton of drills to gain the benefit of speed training.

- The off-season phase of training should concentrate on resisted drills, hills, and stadium stairs along with acceleration and top-speed work. Starts and acceleration with minimal top-speed sprinting are sufficient for in-season purposes.

- General strength and power training will help advance your speed development.

A simple way to put together a plan for the week (7 days) is to first decide what will be the toughest workouts for the week and then insert recovery and lighter technique around those hard days. Following is an example of a sequence for an off-season phase to help get you started with speed training.

Day 1—Acceleration and hill/resisted sprints

Day 2—Starts

Day 3—Stride (length) and turnover (frequency)

Day 4—OFF

Day 5—Starts

Day 6—Acceleration with the ball

Day 7—OFF

SPEED TRAINING WARM-UP

As mentioned earlier, when performing speed drills, make sure your body is properly warmed up to avoid pulls or strains. Your warm-up should concentrate on activating the striking pattern of the legs during sprinting. This includes active stretches and movement drills that specifically link the feet, calves, hamstrings, and hips as a working unit. Following is a sample routine designed for top-end speed training.

Warm-Up for Top-Speed Drills (use 20 meters)

1. Jog down and back.
2. Walking knee hug into a forward lunge (see chapter 3).

3. Walking alternating leg swings. March forward while holding the arms up overhead. Alternate swinging the legs forward from the hips, attempting to reach the opposite hand.

4. Walking Mach A drill. March down the field with a tall posture using the proper arm and leg position (arm cocked with the thumbs rotated up, elbow back, lead knee bent with the toe flexed up and the bottom foot extended). Concentrate on maintaining good posture throughout. Jog back to your starting point and repeat.

5. Skipping A drill. Using the same posture as the previous drill, perform the A drill with a skip. This should be more tempo dominant than height driven. Jog back to the starting point and repeat.

6. Running A drill. Like the Mach and skipping A drills, use the same posture but run, working to get your feet up and down as many times as possible. Jog back to the starting point and repeat.

7. Walking B drill. This will be the second phase of the Mach series of posture drills. March forward using the A technique. When you reach the top of the drive portion for the lead leg, extend the lower leg (from the knee to the foot) to a position out in front. As you bring the lead foot to the ground, make sure it hits down under the hip and does not slap out in front of you (this will have a braking effect on your running). Continue cycling the leg through to recover for the next step. Jog back to the starting point and repeat.

8. Skipping B drill. This is the previous B drill, only in a skipping fashion. Jog back to the starting point and repeat.

9. Running B drill. Make sure the recovery leg strikes down and through the hip. Repeat.

STARTING MECHANICS

Before covering specific drills, let's look at the ideal body position for overcoming inertia (a ground reactive force) and developing an explosive start. Overcoming inertia, or putting your body in motion, is done by exerting force into the ground in the opposite direction from which you want to move. This is accomplished by creating the proper pushing angle with your body posture. This body angle allows you to apply as much force as possible during each step to get you moving. After describing each element of the starting position, we describe a basic lead-in drill that can be performed as a starting point. Developing this technique will form the foundation to performing various speed drills and give you the ability to apply those drills to the multidirectional speed situations that occur in the game.

Posture

As mentioned earlier, the position of your body is the key to starting. Your body must create positive angles beginning at the ankle and shin. A positive angle refers to a forward lean keeping your torso tall and tight. This puts your body in position to apply force into the ground to get your engine started. The body angle should be about 45 degrees before you actually move, and the lean is created by bending the foot at the ankle, not by bending at the waist. Keep your head neutral to avoid falling forward, which will unbalance you as you move.

Lead-In Drill—Lean-Fall-Go. Stand with your feet together and your body tall, eyes looking forward. Your arms are relaxed and hanging down the side of your body. Start by raising your heels off the ground by doing a calf raise. At the top of the raise, begin to fall forward by bending at the ankle (figure 7.1). You will begin to lose your balance. When you cannot keep yourself from falling, step out, keeping your body in the position to push your feet down and behind your hips. Lean about 45 degrees before takeoff. Progress this drill from walking out to an actual full-speed takeoff. This drill can be part of the warm-up session before any type of acceleration or agility training.

Figure 7.1   Lean-fall-go.

Arm Movement

Keep your arms in a cocked position at nearly 90 degrees. Your hands should be rotated out with your thumbs up in a vertical position. Your arms should be used as a lever to apply force from your upper body. The rotation of your arms is created through your shoulders, by swinging them down and back. This should be a violent action when initiating explosive movement. The arm's range should be from the chin to the hip pocket area.

Lead-In Drill—Big to Little Arm Swings. Stand tall with your feet together and your arms down by your sides. Keep your hands flat with your thumbs facing forward. This will put your thumbs in a vertical position when your arms move forward. This will also keep your elbows from rotating outward, causing excessive rotation. (This can be a tough concept to grasp because it is natural to accelerate on the ball by fending off an opponent with your arms.) Begin the drill by swinging your arms back and forth as wide as you can. Create the movement by rotating through your shoulders and not your elbows (as in banging a drum; figure 7.2*a*). This is the action you want to feel in your upper body when starting or accelerating. After about 10 seconds, begin to bend your elbows slightly as you gradually shorten the length of your swings. Continue to reduce the swinging distance as you increase the speed to produce short, quick, and explosive movements. The range of your swing should now be from the chin to the hip pocket (figure 7.2*b*). Remember, the premise of the drill is to feel movement through the shoulders.

Figure 7.2 *(a)* Big to *(b)* little arm swings.

Leg Drive

The legs are the lower-body mechanism for applying force into the ground. Create the proper driving angles by keeping your drive knee up and your foot cocked. The action should be pistonlike (up and down like an engine piston), and you should strike the ground with your foot hitting behind your hip. This must be an aggressive striking action (short and quick) to put as much force as possible into the ground.

Lead-In Drill—Stationary Leg Drive Wall Drill. Stand in front of a wall with hands on the wall and your arms extended out in front to hold your body up in a forward leaning position. You should create the driving angle with your body to be able to strike the ground down and back. Start by raising one leg with your knee at waist level and your foot flexed. The back heel should be off the ground slightly, helping the hips to stay tall. From this position, begin by driving the raised leg forcefully into the ground, while bringing the opposite knee up and out. Hold this position for

Figure 7.3 Stationary leg drive wall drill.

a few seconds; then continue to exchange legs back and forth, checking your posture through each movement. Make sure as you move that your upper body doesn't begin to raise up, causing you to lose the effect of pushing the ground behind your body (no vertical force). This drill can progress from a stationary hold to a continuous up-and-down pattern for a set time. If you are on the field, position a teammate in front of you so you can lean against her body by placing your hands in front of her shoulders (figure 7.3).

SPEED DRILLS

Once you understand and master these technical positions, begin putting your technique together with drills to gain starting speed and acceleration. These drills should progress from stationary starts to speed-changing sprint drills that mimic game play. Perform these drills when you are fresh, at the beginning of the training session, so you can perform them with high intensity. In addition, resisted speed and top-end speed drills are presented along with a speed-emphasized warm-up routine. A later section on designing a soccer speed program will help you sort out proper drill sequencing.

Starts and Acceleration

In general, use a distance of 10 to 15 meters for starting drills. Explode off the line, gradually slow down, and then walk back to reset for the next repetition. When performing multiple sets, take a short recovery break before starting again.

Basic Start Drills

- *Staggered feet.* Stand with one foot in front of the other in a heel–toe relationship (figure 7.4a).
- *Lateral (side) step.* Stand parallel to the starting line. Step with the foot closest to the line and the toe pointed in the intended direction (figure 7.4b). Rotate your head and shoulders around quickly while using the normal arm swing to generate speed as you move forward.
- *Diagonal step.* Using a staggered foot position, drive off the back foot and step in a short diagonal step either right or left (figure 7.4c). As the back foot comes through, square up your shoulders and accelerate.
- *Reverse drop step.* Stand facing away from the starting line and accelerate by dropping the right or left foot, opening your hips and using your arms to get moving (figure 7.4d).

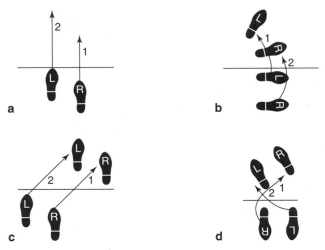

Figure 7.4   Foot placement for *(a)* staggered feet, *(b)* lateral step, *(c)* diagonal step, and *(d)* reverse drop step.

Intermediate Start Drills

Get-Up

This is another method to accentuate the drive mode of acceleration. Lie facedown with your arms bent and your hands flat on the ground. Using a starting signal (whistle, verbal command, or visual, such as a ball passed ahead of you), get your body off the ground quickly by driving your knees up toward your chest and begin to turn your feet over. Once again, you will need to generate force with your arms as you move forward. You can vary this drill by starting on your back and rolling right or left to get up, or on your side as if you have gone into a tackle.

Get Up and Chase   ◉ *DVD*

Lie in a prone position with a partner or teammate directly behind you and about 2 meters between you both (your partner's head should be 2 meters from your feet). On command, both of you get up as quickly as possible and accelerate about 25 meters. Your partner attempts to catch and tag you before you reach the finish line. Change positions on the next repetition. You can vary the starting positions just like in the previous drill.

Advanced Start Drills

Hop or Jump and Go   ◉ *DVD*

These drills are also acceleration dominant but with a higher intensity level. They put stress on the coupling or switching aspect involved in plyometrics. This action refers to the ability to change from an eccentric (lengthening) loaded position to a concentric (shortening) position in a short period of time. The goal is to perform an explosive movement, briefly gain control, and stop; then accelerate quickly.

- *Two forward jumps, one jump back, and accelerate.* Jump out off both feet (broad jump) for distance; you should be under control and balanced when you land. Upon landing, perform another jump forward. After sticking the second jump, take a jump backward and then quickly accelerate for 15 meters. Concentrate on a fast transition from one movement to the next.

- *Lateral jump and accelerate.* Face perpendicular to your targeted direction. Jump sideways with both feet out as far as possible and absorb the ground with soft knees when landing. Jump back to the starting area and then open your head, shoulders, and hips in your intended direction. Once again, sprint full speed for 15 meters. Perform the next repetition facing the opposite way.

- *Diagonal jump and accelerate.* Jump with both feet together in a diagonal direction right or left. Land softly and repeat for a total of four jumps. After the fourth jump, take a 45-degree step forward in the opposite direction from which you landed (if you land to the right, step diagonally left, and vice versa) and accelerate.

- *180-degree turn and go.* Stand and face opposite of your intended direction. Jump vertically, turning in the air either right or left, and land softly. Put good effort into the jump first and then accelerate explosively. You can also perform a simulated or actual (with the ball) header in the air to make it more specific.

- *270- or 360-degree turn and go.* Repeat the 180-degree turn and go drill, but continue turning to a three-quarter or full turn position. Maximize your jump in the air and then accelerate.

- *Single-leg hop and go.* Hop off one foot forward for two jumps. As you land, hop backward once and then accelerate for 15 meters. Maintain control when landing while keeping the knee soft (slightly bent). Repeat the drill on the opposite leg. Vary the drill by hopping laterally (sideways).

Medicine Ball Throw and Chase

Like in the medicine ball throws presented in chapter 6, the resistance of the ball in these drills creates explosive power that will add momentum to your start. Use a ball that weighs between 3 and 4 kilograms (7 to 9 lb.). Release the ball and accelerate downfield to chase past the moving ball.

- *Push and go.* Squat with the ball at chest height to load your hips. Unload the ball by extending your legs and torso and carrying the momentum out through your hands. Jump forward as you release the ball. As you land, accelerate quickly past the ball.

- *Scoop toss and go.* Load your hips and legs by squatting down and bringing the ball between your feet. Extend your hips and legs forcefully and release the ball up and out as you jump forward. Work to get good extension through your arms and hands. Accelerate as in the previous start.

- *Side rotation and go.* Stand perpendicular to the direction in which you will release the ball and load your back hip and leg (if rotating to the right, load the left leg and hip). Rotate your upper body with the ball forcefully, using the momentum of the ball, to project the ball up and out as it takes your feet off the ground. Land softly and begin to accelerate using a lateral step and rotating your hips, shoulders, and head in the intended running direction.

- *Over the back and go.* Stand facing the opposite direction from which you will release the ball. Load your body through your hips by squatting down and bringing the ball toward the ground between your feet. Explode through your legs and hips, bringing the ball up and over your head. Release the ball over your head, finishing with your arms fully extended. The momentum should take your feet off the ground. Land on your feet and immediately drop your right or left foot, open your shoulders and hips in the same direction in which you released the ball, and accelerate quickly.

Resisted Speed Drills

Another way to improve the driving phase of acceleration and stride frequency is to add resistance by changing the running surface (sand or water), changing the surface angle (using a ramp or hill), or towing (using a sled, speed cord, or partner resistance). This type of work is a great way to get your feet up and down quickly while maintaining the proper body angles to drive your body forward.

Resisted speed drills can be very taxing and should be arranged with the proper protocols (repetitions and rest periods), keeping the distance short and brief, but intense. Keep in mind that the amount of resistance doesn't need to be extreme to exhibit a training effect. I've seen coaches increase the load too much because the athlete doesn't look like he is struggling enough, resulting in the drill becoming slower and the technique deteriorating. I like to have athletes tow between 10 and 20 percent of their body weight (a 150 lb. [68 kg] athlete would tow between 15 and 30 lb. [6.8-13.6 kg]). This doesn't need to be exact, but select a load that doesn't result in a significant loss of tempo (resisted fast versus slow motion fast). The same holds true for hills and inclined surfaces. Typically, you want to use an incline of around 10 degrees for maintaining good sprinting mechanics. The steeper the incline becomes, the slower the movement will become, and the transfer will be less effective. Doing speed drills in a sandpit will decrease your traction and eliminate a quick rebound as you move. This mode of training will force your body to adjust by activating more stabilizing and core muscles. This should give you the sensation of more structure strength and efficiency when sprinting on a regular surface. You can also perform the hops, jumps, and bounds presented in chapter 6 to receive the same type of effect.

Sled Towing or Speed Cord Towing

Find an open field with natural or artificial grass. This area should be around 50 to 60 yards long with a flat, level surface. Use a sled-pulling apparatus that can hold a metal or rubber weight secured to the base. A resistance cord should be attached at the front of the sled, and the opposite end should be secured by a belt locked around your waist. Always double-check to make sure all parts of the sled and belt are in working order and secure before attempting any towing drills. Align yourself in front of the sled, moving forward enough to take out any of the slack of the towing cord. Adopt a staggered stance with your feet, and adjust your arms and hands to the correct starting stance as mentioned earlier. Keep looking out 3 to 4 feet (90 to 120 cm) in front in the intended running direction.

To start, explode with your arms, hips, and feet to generate as much force as possible into the ground to get the resistance moving. This initial start should feel like you are attacking the ground with your feet. Avoid popping your head upright at this point to eliminate the resistance pulling you backward. As you begin to generate speed, use good sprinting technique (posture, arm swing, and leg drive) to finish the designated running distance (figure 7.5). Gradually slow down under control to stop the drill. Recover for the prescribed time and repeat. After completing the resisted repetitions, perform 2 or 3 repetitions without the resistance. You should feel the sensation of being lighter and faster.

Figure 7.5 Sled towing.

Hill or Ramp Sprints

Find a hill or ramp that inclines to around 10 degrees and is between 30 and 60 yards in length. The surface can be grass, concrete, or asphalt, but understand that a steady diet of harder surfaces can lead to overuse injuries including shin splints and stress fractures, so mix it up! Start the exercise at the base of the incline using the same starting position as with sled towing. The gradual incline will force you to pick your feet up quickly and then get them back down just as quickly, which is great for turnover. Concentrate on accelerating through the resistance (inclined surface) as you run to the peak. This drill requires that you use a forceful arm swing. Recover from each sprint by walking backward down the incline to stretch both calf and ankle muscles.

Stair Sprints

Locate stadium or walkway stairs that are around 30 yards in distance and have steps that are wide enough to place your whole foot on securely. Check the stairs to make sure they are safe and clear of debris. Start at the bottom of the staircase and accelerate up using good sprinting mechanics. Make sure your knee is driven up with your foot flexed and elbows cocked while maintaining a tall posture. Concentrate on keeping the speed of the run the same all the way to the top, especially at the end when fatigue may break down your technique. Recover between sprints by walking down the stairs, rest 30 seconds at the bottom, and then repeat. Perform 1 or 2 sets of 8 to 10 repetitions.

Top-End Speed Drills

Starting speed and acceleration are a necessity in the game of soccer. Your training time and attention should be primarily spent in this mode of speed development. However, eventually you will want to open up your stride to full-speed sprinting. You should be ready from the beginning after developing running mechanics, but you should work on sprinting in conjunction with accelerating and starting. This is where top-end speed drills come into play. They are designed to help you develop maximal speed that can be applied on the field when you are called on to make a full-speed run that is more than just a short acceleration.

Two speed components come into play here: stride frequency and stride length. They work together to create top-end mechanics for maintaining maximal speed. Stride frequency relates to a quick, productive turnover of the legs in which you feel as though you are floating across the running surface. Stride length (the length of each stride) will increase as you move from acceleration to full-speed running. Fine-tuning these two speed components will improve your sprinting efficiency in the game.

The drills listed here can be inserted as part of speed workouts, after acceleration work, or as a separate focal point of a complementary workout. Keep in mind that before performing full-speed drills, you must have a proper warm-up because of both the intensity (full speed) and the nature of the movement (lengthening and the impact on the ground). Your warm-up should include an active stretch period in which the hips, hamstrings, hip flexors, and calf–ankle complex are addressed.

Sprint-In, Sprint-Out

Use an open field or running track of 100 to 120 meters. Make sure the surface is level and free of any obstacles. Set a marker (cones or agility poles) at measured points of 30 meters, 70 meters, and 90 meters from your designated starting mark. After you have completed your warm-up, position yourself at the start and begin by gradually building up speed so that by the time you reach the first marker (30 meters) you have reached full speed. Continue through the next zone (30 to 70 meters) by concentrating on a fast turnover with your arms and legs using good sprint mechanics (tall posture, toes up, knees driving forward, arms cocked, and eyes focused ahead). Be explosive with each step to get maximum rebound from ground contact. As you pass the end of the zone, begin to gradually decelerate, using the last zone (70 to 90 meters) to stop under control.

S-Curve Runs 💿 📀

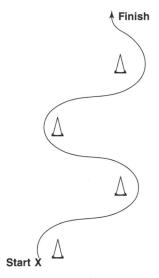

This drill incorporates running full speed in and out of a slight curve. It simulates a player making an overlap type of run to gain position when attacking the goal. Use a running area between 60 and 100 meters and space markers (tall cones or agility poles) anywhere from 15 to 25 meters as indicated (figure 7.6). Accelerate forward and begin to weave in and out of the markers at full speed. Lean into and explode out of the curve as you progress down the field. To vary the drill, position a teammate 5 meters away, standing shoulder to shoulder. Designate one of you as "the leader" and the other as "the reactor." Begin running down the field with the leader running a curve pattern and the reactor simulating the same pattern without losing the 5-meter cushion between you. Repeat the drill and switch running roles.

Figure 7.6   S-curve runs.

Focusing on soccer-specific speed development can give you an extra advantage when challenged in game situations. Increasing your speed can elevate your play to a new level in terms of the other components as well. Chapter 8 will take these basic speed techniques and transfer them to change of direction and quickness, also known as agility.

Agility

The development of straight-ahead speed technique can obviously improve your performance on the field when needing to get from one point to another fast. But the game of soccer is not always played in a straight line, and you may never get to full speed before the next change of direction arises. As mentioned in chapter 1, soccer players are asked to move at full speed, stop under control, and then reaccelerate in the opposite direction many times during competition. For this reason you need techniques that will improve your agility and quickness.

Agility is the ability to react to a situation swiftly while coordinating quick starts and stops under control to make a play. Efficiency in this component is critical to success on the field because of the unpredictability of many team sports, including soccer. Learning how to control your body in space will not only help you to react quicker to these unpredictable events, but it will also get you into position to create positive plays for your team.

Agility is evident throughout the game of soccer in many skills, from dribbling to passing and trapping. Creating and defending space on the field is a constant battle, and agility is a big part of that battle. Like speed, agility can be improved. The great thing is that, because of the neuromuscular nature of agility training, you will notice changes in these skills almost immediately. I've seen marked improvement in foot speed and quickness in just a few workouts. The key is to increase the speed of the drill only when you have mastered the technique to avoid rehearsing bad technique.

AGILITY ESSENTIALS

Along with accelerating, agility involves reaction time, balance, coordination, stopping, and starting. Agility drills can be either reactive or nonreactive. Nonreactive drills are those in which the athlete can anticipate what is going to happen, whereas reactive drills require the athlete to react to a stimulus and make a split-second decision. Both reactive and nonreactive drills will improve your agility, but as a soccer player you should focus on reactive drills. These are most likely to transfer to the game. The following agility essentials form the framework for designing a training routine for increasing your quickness and ability to change direction.

• **Reaction time**—Reaction time is the time it takes to recognize and react to a stimulus. The stimulus can be visual, auditory, or kinesthetic. All three are present in a soccer game. Seeing the ball in play serves as a visual cue to where the game is happening. How fast you can track the ball or locate an opponent will determine how well you make plays. As a defender, hearing your keeper from behind bark out instructions is critical for creating a solid defense. Anticipating action and feeling or moving off an opponent's pressure are qualities of players with good reaction time. You can decrease your reaction time by performing drills that use all types of stimulation and are specific to the game. Drills in which you must react to a partner or the ball will be most helpful for transferring your skills to the game.

Being able to change directions quickly and maneuver around obstacles such as other players requires excellent agility skills.

©Scott Bales/Icon SMI

• **Balance**—Keeping your center of mass over your feet is important when transitioning from one movement to the next. Your center of mass is located typically just above the hips. Balance requires that you lower your body under control so you can sustain good posture for movement in any direction. Cutting drills demand more dynamic balance than basic footwork drills, but all good athletic movements require active balance throughout the body.

• **Coordination**—Coordination involves producing several

movements together in a seamless way. Soccer play is full of coordinated ball skills on the ground and in the air that when put together produce all-star-caliber play. To improve coordination, perform each agility drill at a slower rate to develop technical proficiency before introducing speed. Agility also requires coordination between the lower body and upper body when moving in space. The arms play a role in balancing the upper body while adjusting the center of gravity for the next move.

• **Stopping**—Being able to stop quickly with control will enhance multidirectional speed changes during the game. This skill is strength dominated, and a deficiency in lower-body and core strength will affect your ability to regain your balance on the move. Stopping mechanics need to be rehearsed through all three planes of motion to mimic game-like situations. Developing good stopping mechanics is especially crucial for women because they are more likely to experience ACL injury. Why women suffer more ACL injuries than men has been a topic of discussion for a while. Research has suggested various causes, such as weak hamstrings, hormone differences, hip width differences, and altered muscle firing patterns. Building total-body strength and practicing drills that teach stopping will help to minimize injury.

• **Starting**—Acceleration work through starting drills (see chapter 7) can improve your ability to move in various directions while reacting to a partner or the ball. Incorporating explosive bursts of speed during the agility drills will eliminate any lag when changing directions. These starts should include moving forward, backward, and sideways; rotating; and moving at different angles.

DRILL SELECTION FOR AGILITY TRAINING

When designing an agility and quickness program for soccer, keep in mind that movements are meant to be explosive, fast, and to the point. Thus, it's important to perform agility training when you are fresh, such as at the start of a training session or after some light technical or skill training. It is also important to remember that the drills should not be very long in duration, and the total volume of exercises should be minimal to maintain a high-speed training environment. Make sure you have proper footwear that supports your feet well, especially near the ankle, and good traction.

I like to start each agility session with at least one footwork drill to get the session off to a fast pace. Depending on the particular drill, perform 2 or 3 sets using an 8- to 10-second time frame to execute as many repetitions as possible. Incorporate as much speed as you can control, and recover between sets to keep the intensity as high as possible.

Once the footwork segment is finished, continue the session with 5 to 8 starts to stimulate the fast starting action of the agility drills. Then, choose 2 or 3 agility drills focusing on change of direction, cutting, cone or hurdle work, or reaction, and perform no more than 6 repetitions of each.

Most agility training should be performed during the off-season, when you can spend time on proper technique. During the season, use agility as a way to stimulate the brain and the muscles for match readiness. These sessions should be shorter with less total volume.

As fatigue sets in, the tempo of the drills will begin to diminish. Fatigue and a visible change in tempo can help you determine when to end an agility training session. If you continue past the point of fatigue, poor mechanics take over and the training becomes counterproductive.

Drills for building agility range from foot speed maneuvers to on-field partner-reaction changes of direction. Choose activities that will be challenging as well as those that address your individual needs. Remember that with agility training a little can go a long way, so use drills that have a purpose and a progression. Let's look at the drills associated with soccer agility.

FOOT SPEED DRILLS

Line Drills

Create a tape or chalk line on a nonslick surface. Perform the designated footwork for 8 to 10 seconds as fast as possible with control. With each step your foot should be slightly off the ground, eliminating any sliding or dragging. Coordinate the arm action with the stepping mechanics (for forward and backward movements, the arms should be in opposition to the feet, just like in walking or running).

- *Forward and backward shuffle.* Start with one foot over the line and one foot behind. Begin moving back and forth, tapping your toes quickly, while moving your arms in opposition. Your feet should make a tapping sound and not be sliding on the ground.

- *Alternating single step (forward and backward).* Alternate stepping over the line and back, as in a "running in place" style of moving. Don't forget to use your arms to increase your speed.

- *Alternating crossovers.* Using a straddle start, begin by bouncing and crossing one foot over the line while the opposite foot crosses behind. Continue moving back and forth, switching your lead foot. Turn and rotate your hips as your feet cross over.

Line Drills Using Reaction

Using an auditory command, you can add reactive response to the line drills. A partner or teammate, or even your coach, can help you improve your reaction time.

- Stand with both feet in front of the line and begin chopping your feet in place. On the "right" or "left" command, tap the designated foot over the line quickly and continue to move your feet in place.
- Line up with both feet facing either to the left or right of the line. Like before, chop your feet in place and react to the "go" command by tapping the foot closest to the line (lateral step) over and back quickly.
- Another variation is using the same starting position as the previous drill, but instead of a lateral step, use a crossover step.

Cross Drill

This is another footwork drill that is similar to the line drill. Draw or tape two intersecting lines to form a cross with four equal quadrants. The top left quadrant is designated Q-1. The top right is Q-2. The bottom right is Q-3, and the bottom left is Q-4. Begin by standing with both feet in Q-2 and hop quickly back and forth from Q-2 to Q-3 for about 10 seconds. Count the number of contacts in 10 seconds and progress from this point. Other combinations include 1-2, 1-3, 2-4, 1-2-3, 1-2-4, 1-2-3-4, 1-4-3-2, and 1-2-4-3. Once the patterns are established, try performing on one foot to challenge your dynamic balance as well. Remember to build speed as you develop confidence with your footwork.

Advance this drill by adding a starting sprint (10 yd.) after 5 seconds of the quick foot drill. Be fast with your feet and explosive in the start.

ABC Ladder Drills

The ABC ladder was designed as a portable way to develop quick feet. It consists of a series of 1-by-1-foot plastic squares connected to a folding cord that can be laid out on the ground. The ABC acronym stands for agility, balance, and coordination, which are the essence of all athletic movements. The key points when performing ladder drills are as follows:

- Move only as fast as you can control your feet. Slower and correct is better than fast and sloppy.
- Coordinate your arm movements in a relaxed manner along with your footwork. A tense upper body usually translates into out-of-control movement.
- Use soft-stepping, light feet rather than heavy, pounding feet.

With ladder drills, if you use your imagination, the list is endless. I like to start with a basic series that involves the main movement patterns found in team sports. After developing these patterns, you can start to deviate into other combinations and add starts to the finish. Following is a description of the basic routine.

Agility Ladder Patterns

- *One in—forward.* Face the end of the ladder and, with proper running form, put one foot in each square and pump your arms *(a)*.

- *Two in—forward.* Use the same procedure as the preceding, except with two feet in each square *(b)*. Alternate starting the drill with the right and left foot.

- *Two in—lateral.* Move sideways through the ladder while putting each foot in the square *(c)*. Alternate lead legs. Focus on keeping your shoulders, hips, and feet parallel to the ladder.

- *Diagonal step: one in, one out—forward.* Start facing forward at either side of the ladder, and diagonally shuffle into the middle of the ladder with both feet; then step out to the other side with one foot *(d)*. With the other foot, immediately shuffle back in the opposite direction and repeat the pattern.

- *Diagonal step: one in, one out—backward.* Just like in the previous drill, start on one side or the other of the ladder, but face away from it. Perform the same step sequence as with the preceding, but move backward *(e)*. Make sure you open your lead hip to be able to drop-step quickly. This is a good drill to master when playing defense or as a keeper.

- *Forward step: in-out-out.* Face forward at the end of the ladder and step either foot into the first square. Bring the opposite foot in next. Now move your lead foot to the outside of the same square, and finally, bring your trail foot to the other side *(f)*. This should look like a hopscotch pattern, but with stepping instead of hopping.

- *Lateral step: one in, one out—down the side.* Start facing the ladder on one side or the other and bring your lead foot (the foot closest to the first square of the ladder) into the ladder *(g)*. (If you are moving to the right, then your right foot goes into the lead square as you move down the line.) Continue down the line (alternating one foot in while the other steps back) moving your arms back and forth as though you were running. Lead with the opposite foot on the way back.

- *Lateral shuffle—down the side.* This is similar to the previous drill only with the feet shuffling instead of stepping *(h)*. Use short, quick toe taps as you move sideways. The arm action stays the same as before.

- *Crossover step forward.* Start to the side on one end of the ladder facing forward and begin by crossing the outside foot in front of your body, landing in the first square. Move to the other side of the ladder and place both feet on the outside of the ladder. Only the lead foot will actually touch in the next square *(i)*. Keep moving forward with your hips rotating quickly to get your lead foot over and down on the ground.

(a) One in—forward.

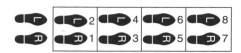

(b) Two in—forward.

(c) Two in—lateral.

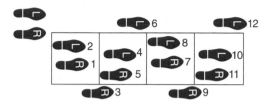

(d) Diagonal step: one in, one out—forward.

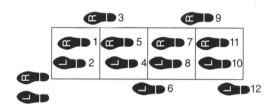

(e) Diagonal step: one in, one out—backward.

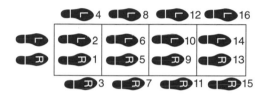

(f) Forward step: in-out-out.

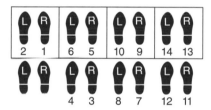

(g) Lateral step: one in, one out—down the side.

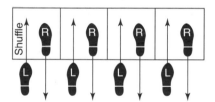

(h) Lateral shuffle—down the side.

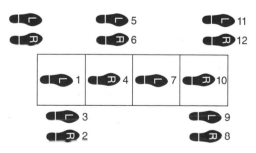

(i) Crossover step forward.

- *Crossover step backward.* Use the foot pattern from the previous drill, but face away from the ladder *(j)*. Cross the lead foot in front of your body as you step into the first square. Drop-step back with the trail foot down to the side of the next square and begin the sequence again using that foot first.

- *Hopscotch.* Face forward at the beginning square and simultaneously hop with both feet into the middle of the square. Hop out with both feet—one on each side of the same square *(k)*. Continue the pattern to the end of the ladder.

- *Two-foot side hops—down the side.* Move through the ladder by hopping with both feet in and out of the squares as you proceed forward *(l)*. You will work down one side of the ladder and then back up the other side.

- *Two-foot hops—zigzag pattern.* Hop into the first square with both feet and then hop out on the other side of the ladder *(m)*. Move in a zigzag pattern through the ladder with a quick bounce. This can also be advanced by performing the pattern hopping on one foot.

Add some basic hops or jumps to your ladder work at the end of your session to generate some low-level explosive training.

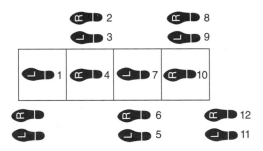

(j) Crossover step backward.

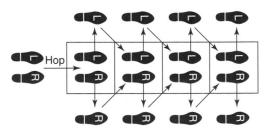

(k) Hopscotch.

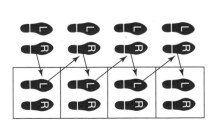

(l) Two-foot side hops—down the side.

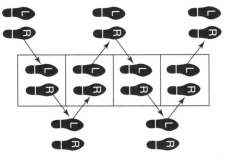

(m) Two-foot hops—zigzag pattern.

Minihurdles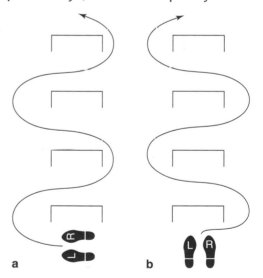

Set six to eight minihurdles (6 in., or 15 cm, high) 2 feet (60 cm) apart. Hurdle work mimics line work with the addition of height. As with the line drills, keep the stepping patterns quick but soft, and continue using your upper torso and arms to synchronize your total body. The minihurdles can add variety to your footwork development.

- *Lateral stepping.* Start at one end and quickly move sideways down the hurdles, keeping your feet, hips, and shoulders parallel to the hurdles. Move your arms back and forth to provide extra tempo to the drill; they should match the speed of your feet.

- *Crossover step: two in.* Move sideways as before, but lead with a crossover step over each hurdle. Bring the trail foot down to the ground before moving over the next hurdle. Keep the upper body facing forward as with the lateral step.

- *Crossover step: one in.* This is the same as the previous crossover drill except that you alternate hurdles with each step. The trail foot will not step down after the lead foot steps over the hurdle; rather, it will go over the next hurdle.

- *Forward and backward shuffle.* Move forward shuffling your feet quickly (the hurdle will be to the side of your feet; use it as a marker to work around). Shuffle one step sideways, and then quickly change to a backpedal step to move past the next hurdle in line *(a)*. Continue this back-and-forth movement through the series of hurdles, working a fast change of direction.

- *Forward and backward side shuffle.* Facing the row of hurdles, shuffle to the right using the first hurdle as a marker to maneuver around. Slide back to the left between this and the next hurdle, and continue this pattern throughout the course *(b)*. When you reach the end of the hurdles, move with a backward shuffle down the hurdles until you return to the starting point.

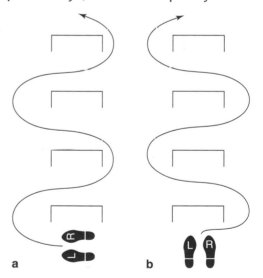

Minihurdle footwork: *(a)* forward and backward shuffle and *(b)* forward and backward side shuffle.

- *Two-foot lateral hopping.* Hop sideways with both feet with just enough air time to clear the hurdle. These hops should be quick with short ground contact times between hurdles. You can add a twist to the jumps by rotating in the air after the last hurdle and continue hopping back in the opposite direction.
- *Hurdle sampler.* Combine all of the movements into one set and see how fast you can change from one move to the next. Here is a sample sequence: lateral stepping, forward and backward shuffle, side shuffle, and, finally, two-foot lateral hopping. Try various combinations, and even add a quick acceleration after the last move!

STOPPING DRILLS

Stopping mechanics are critical to change of direction because of the amount of loading that occurs on the ankles, knees, and hips while performing on the field. Overall strength, especially in the legs and core, will help you eccentrically control unexpected changes in play. Slowing down the movement to feel your legs and hips load will give you the muscle memory to stabilize during live action. As mentioned in chapter 5, soccer players should be involved in a well-planned, progressive strength training program to develop the necessary strength for efficient movement. The legs are your base of support that will, along with your core, stabilize your dynamic posture on the field. When you can execute the basic loading drill well, move to more dynamic and challenging ways to improve agility.

Oregon Shift Drill

This exercise, also described in chapter 3 and found in the Flexibility section of the DVD, is a great way to introduce proper loading of the legs, which you will have to do during a brief stop in movement. This drill will help you understand how to transfer your center of mass by using your hips.

Stand with your feet outside your shoulders and squat as deeply as possible. Hold a 12-inch (30 cm) cone in each hand, and, reaching out as far as you can without raising your feet off the ground, place one cone on the ground. Do the same with the other cone. Then lean and reach to one side to touch the cone. Shift your weight back to the other side and touch that cone. Continue shifting back and forth to complete a total of 10 repetitions.

Wheel Drill   ◉ DVD

This drill, designed by Vern Gambetta, is based on a movement series that uses the three planes of motion to accelerate and slow down momentum. Use an open space in which you can maneuver five steps in any direction. Imagine that you are standing in the center of a wheel and that each step corresponds to a spoke on the wheel. Move by stepping out to the front and to the side as well as rotating back to load and stabilize from one foot to the other. The last step is a balancing step that you hold from 1 to 5 seconds depending on the number of steps taken. Go back to the center between spokes. The progression of steps moves from one step to three steps to an active five steps. An example of the three-step move would be, starting with the left foot, stepping left, right, and left, and holding the final step for 3 seconds. This would occur all the way around the wheel until you are back to the starting point. Increase to the five-step level only when your stability has improved.

Reactive Stop and Go

This is an intermediate-level stopping drill that uses an auditory command. Position yourself at the beginning of 50 yards of field space. On the "go" command, accelerate downfield. When you hear a "stop" command, gain control as fast as possible and freeze in an athletic stance (knees bent and hips down). You should take only a minimal number of steps before coming to a full stop. Hold the pause position for 2 counts. On the second "go" command, reaccelerate down the field once again. You can use any number of stops and changes as you become more efficient. Include backpedaling and accelerations to the sides and with angles.

CUTTING DRILLS

Once you understand stopping mechanics, progress to a basic cutting drill to quicken your time through agility tests and drill training. Cutting is the ability to plant either your outside foot to make an explosive power move or your inside foot to speed-cut around an obstacle. Soccer uses both types.

Outside Foot Cut

Place two cones 8 yards apart at a 45-degree angle from each other. Use a 10-yard buildup start to begin. Continue to the right of the first cone and plant your right foot by bending your body at the ankle, knee, and hip. Explode off the plant leg and accelerate to the next cone on the left. As your body passes the cone, plant the opposite leg (left) and explode back to the right, finishing about 10 yards past the first cone. Don't forget the importance of your arms in generating force to accelerate explosively.

Inside Foot Cut

Using the same cone setup as the outside foot cut drill, run through the cones, this time using the inside foot to make a speed cut (this will have almost a rounding effect if performed correctly). You will have to lean to the inside of the cone to maintain your speed through the cut.

PROGRAMMED AGILITY DRILLS

Programmed agility work should be the base for developing the correct mechanics when changing direction. These drills are predetermined courses that take away most of the reactive component. As you become familiar with the drills and are able to control your posture, begin to move into more reactive drills that can transfer specifically to soccer. Whether you are shuffling, backpedaling, or cutting, keep in mind that your center of mass will change as you change movements. You will need to make constant adjustments to maintain your balance. This is why working a programmed drill in a controlled environment gives you a good understanding of when and where changes of posture are necessary.

Four-Corner Drill

Align four cones in the corners of a 5-by-5-yard square. Start at one corner and execute the designated movements as fast as possible, keeping the changes at the corners quick and sharp (angles). Finish each square with a sprint forward for 5 yards. Perform each sequence from both directions.

Sequence Samples

- Sprint, shuffle, backpedal, shuffle, sprint forward 5 yards
- Backpedal, carioca, sprint, carioca, turn and sprint forward 5 yards
- Side shuffle, sprint, carioca, turn and side shuffle, turn and sprint

Cone Weave

Set sixteen 12-inch (30 cm) cones in four rows of four with 2 feet (60 cm) between the cones and 3 feet (90 cm) between lanes. Start at one corner and work up each row of cones in a quick, shuffling movement to avoid the cones. At the top of the line sprint back to the beginning of the next row of cones and start the process again. When you reach the last row of cones, sprint finish for 5 yards. Advance this drill by shuffling forward down the first row and then shuffling backward down the next row. When you get to the end, two-foot hop over the last row of cones. The objective is to change direction as fast as possible without losing control.

Pro Agility Shuttle

Position two cones 10 yards apart and place a third cone halfway between them. Start by facing the middle cone in an athletic stance. Sprint to the right cone and touch the ground. Sprint back through the start to the opposite cone (left) and touch the ground again. Explode back through the start/finish line.

Compass Drill

Align four cones around a center cone in a north, south, east, and west direction 3 meters from the center cone. Start with your right hand touching the top of the center cone while facing the south cone. On "go," sprint to the east cone, touching it with your left hand. Return to the center cone, touching it with your right hand. Continue this pattern with your left hand to the outside cone and your right hand to the center cone while working around the circle. The sequence should be east-middle-south-middle-west-middle-north-middle (in a clockwise direction). At the last middle cone touch, sprint back past the north cone to finish. Repeat the sequence in the opposite direction (counterclockwise) using your left hand to touch the center cone.

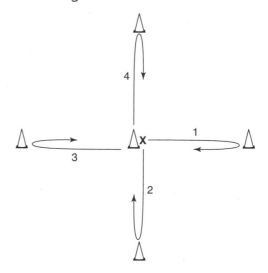

Ajax Shuttle Drill

Set two cones 10 yards apart. Begin by sprinting to the far cone, planting at the cone, and then sprinting back to the starting line. Repeat this shuttle-style sprint for five lengths (50 yd.). Each run should be explosive with a quick turn at the line. A quality time for this drill would be under 10 seconds. Perform 5 to 10 sets using a 30-second rest interval to recover between sets.

T-Drill Runs

Set four agility poles or 12-inch (30 cm) cones in a T formation, with the bottom of the T 5 yards from the middle cone and each side cone 5 yards from the center cone. Begin the drill on the left side of the starting cone at the bottom of the T. Accelerate to the middle cone and make a quick right turn around the cone. Continue sprinting to the right of the side cone and make a left turn around that cone. Move to the center cone, make a left turn toward the finish cone, and pass it. Repeat in the opposite direction. To advance the drill, dribble the ball as you work the pattern; then make a shot as you come out of the drill. To make it more reactive, replace the center cone with a partner and have her call out or point to a direction in which to run the drill. Perform between three and six runs per set and 2 or 3 sets using a 30-second rest interval between runs and around a minute between sets.

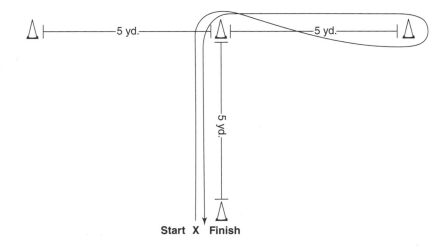

Agility Ladder With Slalom Cone Run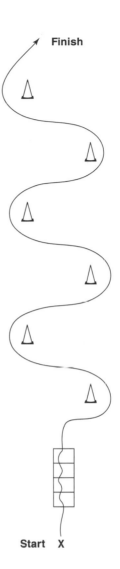

Set up an agility ladder with six to eight 12-inch (30 cm) cones at one end in a zigzag pattern with 8 feet (2.4 m) between cones. Start the run with a 5-yard pickup (jog) to the beginning of the ladder. At the ladder, begin using any combination of foot drills discussed in the preceding agility ladder section. Continue out of the ladder by accelerating to the first cone and plant either the inside or outside foot to cut and accelerate to the next cone. Finish the cones and then sprint 5 yards to stop the drill. Vary the exercise by performing a backward foot drill (e.g., backward diagonal shuffle) to a back shuffle through the cones; then turn and sprint.

REACTIVE DRILLS

Reactive drills constitute the final group of agility drills. This is where you can become as specific as you want because, as a soccer player, performance ultimately comes down to how you react to situations on the field. We have, to this point, discussed the basic techniques involved with agility and quickness, and you know that posture, body control, strength, and the nervous system together form the foundation for increasing reaction time. Decreasing reaction time can be accomplished only by drilling with nondeliberate situations at full speed. Here are a few drill samples presented by positions. Use a variety of stimuli, including vocal, visual, and kinesthetic.

Keepers: Partner Reaction (With Ball)

Lie facedown at the mouth of the goal with your head toward the net. Have a partner stand facing the net at the top of the penalty box with a ball. Have your partner give a "go" command to begin the drill. Upon hearing the command, jump up and face outside the net, keeping your feet moving in place. Your partner then delivers a shot on goal, and you attempt to dive, catch, or deflect the shot. If you catch the shot, clear the ball and then sprint 10 yards to end the drill. If you deflect it, get up or land quickly and execute the 10-yard sprint.

Defenders: Ball Tracking

Put four cones 5 yards apart. To the right of these cones place six more cones at various distances and angles. Number these cones 1 through 6. Start the drill by moving forward and backward quickly between the two cones. On a partner's command, backtrack to the designated cone, plant, and sprint back to the start. Perform three sprints before taking a 45-second rest for a total of 3 to 5 sets.

Forwards: Header Attack

Set a cone 5 yards in front of the 6-yard line. Position your partner in front of the goal with the ball. A third player stands shoulder to shoulder with you at the starting cone, facing away from the goal. The player standing next to you starts the drill by putting pressure (pushing) against your body. Fight the pressure by moving with it and break contact by turning and sprinting to the goal. As you continue to the goal, your partner tosses a ball in the air for you to head into the goal. Jog back after the shot and reset for the next attempt. Vary the next repetition by switching players and having the pressuring player work against the pressure given.

Midfielders: Palmer Drill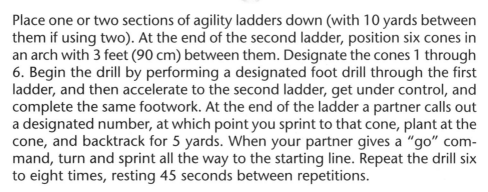

Place one or two sections of agility ladders down (with 10 yards between them if using two). At the end of the second ladder, position six cones in an arch with 3 feet (90 cm) between them. Designate the cones 1 through 6. Begin the drill by performing a designated foot drill through the first ladder, and then accelerate to the second ladder, get under control, and complete the same footwork. At the end of the ladder a partner calls out a designated number, at which point you sprint to that cone, plant at the cone, and backtrack for 5 yards. When your partner gives a "go" command, turn and sprint all the way to the starting line. Repeat the drill six to eight times, resting 45 seconds between repetitions.

Agility and footwork drills are the closest you will come in training to actual field situations. It is important to understand the basic principles of controlling your center of mass, stopping under control, and using correct footwork before performing high-speed agility work. Realize that general overall strength—and specifically, core and lower-body strength—will accelerate your improvement in the areas of quickness and change of direction. As you become more efficient in your agility, devote more time to position-specific, reactive agility training.

Chapter 9

Peak Conditioning for the Game

To this point, we have explored ways to increase the quick, explosive, and power components necessary in soccer. To develop the total soccer athletic package, you will also need specific conditioning to maintain a high-quality performance for the duration of the game. During competition, you have to work through fatigue factors while still performing at a high level. Increasing your fatigue threshold will help you maintain that performance. In one form or another, soccer draws from all energy systems throughout the game—the fast-acting anaerobic system for high-intensity work and the aerobic system for a steady source of energy for longer periods of work. You should consider this combination of energy systems when designing or implementing your training program. This chapter will help you to organize the overall conditioning aspect of your total training program.

Let's begin by addressing what each energy system brings to the table. The anaerobic energy system uses both a stored energy source, mostly in the muscles, and an energy metabolism by-product, lactic acid, to fuel demands depending on the duration of exercise. This system can supply energy quickly and without oxygen, but only for a short period of time. The percentage of anaerobic energy you use will vary depending on your position and your team's style of play. A goalkeeper, for example, will be able to produce energy from this source for a longer period of time because of the limited amount of time spent running, whereas the outside midfielder's anaerobic energy stores may be taxed a lot sooner. Most explosive starts and interval conditioning draw on the anaerobic system. (Interval training consists of repeated runs or sprints mixed with periods of rest.)

As long as the energy system matches the body's demands, energy will be sustained. When demand exceeds energy availability, you enter into an energy debt and soon become fatigued. Except at the very start of exercise, anaerobic energy is fed by lactic acid, a product of anaerobic metabolism, which replenishes the body during high-intensity work. This source can be maintained up to a certain point (around 3 min. if sustained). When training or exercise progresses beyond that point, oxygen is needed to continue the session (i.e., the aerobic system kicks in), but not to the exclusion of the anaerobic system. This is because breaks are naturally built in to a soccer match (walking, jogging, and standing), allowing you to recover and eliminate energy waste products through respiration.

The aerobic system will contribute to energy needs in soccer by sustaining oxygen uptake and increasing aerobic power. Aerobic power relates to the percentage of your aerobic capacity (the maximum amount of oxygen per minute) that you can use for prolonged exercise. Aerobic power helps your sprint ability late in the game, improves your running efficiency, and replenishes energy quickly to the working muscles. Table 9.1 summarizes the basic components of each energy system, and figure 9.1 shows the contributions of the three systems over time.

Table 9.1 Energy Systems

Energy system	Duration availability/ intensity	Rest-to- work ratio	Activity application
Anaerobic (ATP-CP; fast-acting energy stored in the muscles)—no oxygen	0 to 10 sec. max effort/very high	4:1	Start of match or after extended rest period (halftime)
Anaerobic (glycolysis; reusing lactic acid)—no oxygen	>10 sec. to 2 min./ high	3:1 or 2:1	Extended or repetitive sprinting, defensive marking (with rest)
Aerobic—using oxygen	>2 min./low to medium	1:1	Performance at the end of the game or playing for long periods

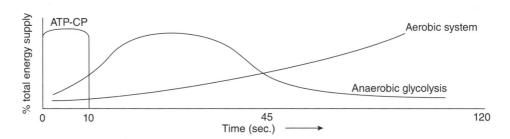

Figure 9.1 Relative contributions of the three energy systems over time.

Reprinted, by permission, from P. Twist, 2007, *Complete conditioning for hockey* (Champaign, IL: Human Kinetics), 56.

Many young players believe that they are moving at full speed for the whole match. With this mind-set, they become "fitness machines" and overwork and overtrain to the point of exhaustion or injury. They can have the same attitude toward conditioning tests. I've seen athletes become consumed in off-season training with one objective—to pass a fitness test. This can lead to diminishing the rest of the athletic qualities to the point of ineffectiveness on the pitch. Video analysis of matches has indicated that the majority of the time players are standing, walking, and jogging rather than engaging in high-intensity sprinting. In fact, most field players spend around half of the total match walking. Compare that to the percentage of game time most players spend standing (15 percent), jogging (25 percent), striding (5 percent), and sprinting (3 percent).

Conditioning for soccer should be done according to a progressive, well-thought-out plan that builds from one phase of training to the next and within the context of the game. Your ability to sustain high speed and power during the late stages of the match will be an advantage when your opponent is fading. The ultimate conditioning goal should be playing at a high rate rather than passing numerous fitness tests. The yearly conditioning plan should involve off-season, preseason, and in-season training goals, because each phase warrants different objectives.

During the off-season, or noncompetitive phase, the emphasis should be on developing baseline conditioning to maintain progress for the next competitive season. This will help you take on more work for performance improvement without getting injured as a result of fatigue. Conditioning should occur more frequently to extend the fatigue threshold and increase the capacity to work at a higher rate.

The extensive conditioning undertaken during the off-season should peak during the preseason cycle of training, typically lasting 2 or 3 weeks, as team practices begin. This is the time to increase the stress of intensive practice sessions and become efficient in your effort. Emphasis is geared to game readiness. Conditioning sessions should be less frequent but of higher quality.

As the competitive season begins, the focus should shift to performance during the match. Maintaining efficient, high-quality fitness to stay sharp for competition is the goal and will help in suppressing the injury rate late in the game. Fitness sessions should be planned around the actual match schedule to keep recoverability high for the next competition. Usually during the season, conditioning is restricted to once a week, unless the time you play in a match is limited (less than 15 min.). Also, conditioning should take place early in the competitive week and no closer than 3 days before a contest. Chapter 12 has examples of how conditioning fits into the program. If quality work is performed during the off- and preseason, this phase should consist of mostly fine-tuning. Add a conditioning session, when time permits, if the time you play in matches is limited.

TRAINING METHODS TO IMPROVE SOCCER CONDITIONING

To achieve the correct training response, you should choose drills that transfer well to the game of soccer. Designing a program according to the anaerobic and aerobic demands of both the position and game will promote improved soccer fitness. Remember, although soccer can last over 90 minutes, the game is always explosive and powerful. Conditioning should reflect this reality. The majority of conditioning time should be focused on intermittent (start and stop) activities with high intensity to mimic match play as closely as possible.

Intensity is the one training variable that will continue to push improvement in your conditioning. Your training heart rate can give you a general marker for improvement. A simple way to use heart rate is to first find your maximum heart rate (MHR). Take the number 220 and subtract your age. This number represents your highest point for exercising safely during a training session. To effectively use this number during training, you need to establish a range to use during the session. For example, if your MHR were 200 bpm (beats per minute), you would need to elevate and sustain your training heart rate between 140 and 160 bpm to train at a range between 70 and 80 percent of your MHR.

How do you know if you are reaching your maximum heart rate range? Heart rate monitors that can be worn on belts or wristbands are now available for use during training sessions. However, an easier approach to calculating heart rate during training is to check your pulse while resting between bouts of effort. You can take your pulse at the carotid artery in your neck, just under the jawline. Use the index and middle finger together, placing slight pressure against the artery. To save time, count the number of beats you feel for 6 seconds, using a stopwatch or wristwatch, and then add a zero to that number. For instance, a reading of 13 beats for 6 seconds would indicate a heart rate of 130 bpm (13 by 10). Using this calculation during training can give you a quick snapshot of your training intensity.

Be aware that your pulse reflects the intensity only after the interval or session has stopped. Technology is beginning to be developed that can capture real-time data including $\dot{V}O_2$max (total oxygen uptake), speed, and distance covered. As your training continues, the intensity level will help you vary your conditioning plan to maintain steady improvement.

CONDITIONING DRILLS

I like to classify soccer conditioning activities into two categories: *general athletic conditioning,* which uses sprint endurance, shuttle-style sprint repeats, and fartlek—or varied-intensity—training; and *soccer-specific conditioning,* which uses position movement pattern training and small-sided games. Choose your category based on your training cycle and competition schedule. Obviously, small-sided games and movement pattern work can be used during the preseason and in-season to simulate the specifics of the game in a controlled environment.

Sprint Endurance Drills

These drills condition sprint ability under fatigue, which is important to most positions late in the match. As with most high-intensity work, these drills should not be repeated on back-to-back training days.

120-Yard Repeats (Intervals)

Using a standard soccer field, begin the drill at the back end line. Have a coach or teammate time the training interval and rest period using a stopwatch. On command, sprint the full length of the field (120 yd.) crossing the finish zone (opposite end line) in 18 seconds (20 sec. for keepers). Upon finishing the sprint, return to the starting zone using a 25-second active recovery (jogging) period. Rest 30 more seconds, and then start the next repetition. Continue, completing 6 repetitions. As your conditioning improves, work up to 10 repetitions in the training session. Try checking your heart rate halfway through the session as well as at the end of the session. This activity will elevate your heart rate into the 80 to 90 percent zone.

Midfield Sprint With Skill Recovery

From the field end line, sprint to midfield (60 yd.) in about 7 or 8 seconds. Recover at midfield (20 sec.) while juggling or dribbling the ball in a designated area (kickoff circle). Repeat the next sprint in the opposite direction, using the penalty box for your skill (shooting) zone. Start with 10 and work up to 15 repetitions.

7-by-30-Meter Sprint Recovery

This drill was presented in chapter 2 as part of the test battery for evaluating sprint recovery. This is also a solid workout during the noncompetitive phases of training. Thirty-meter sprints are repeated seven times with jogging recovery between repetitions.

Six-Minute Run

Preset markers (cones or flags) along the perimeter of the field, spacing them 20 yards apart along the entire area. After a good warm-up, begin the run at one corner of the field, staying to the outside of the markers. Start a stopwatch and continue for 6 minutes. The objective is to cover as much distance as possible for the time period. Record the distance covered to the nearest marker or the last marker you pass (you should measure the total perimeter, in yards or meters, before starting the session). Try not to pace yourself, but just run to see what distance you can cover. To calculate your speed over the distance, take the distance covered and divide by the seconds you have run (6 min. = 360 sec.). For example, if you covered 1,600 yards, the speed rate would be 1,600 yards / 360 seconds = 4.4 yards/second. It would also give you a 264-yard-per-minute running pace (4.4 yd. by 60 sec.) to use for various timed runs in training. This run can be performed every 6 weeks to check improvements in conditioning.

Shuttle-Style Conditioning

This conditioning drill involves completing a designated distance, hitting a touch line, and returning the same distance back to the starting line. Longer distances will be less stressful because the total number of touches will be fewer. Combine both short and longer distances to challenge yourself. Lower your sprint time to increase the intensity.

300-Yard Shuttle

Mark a distance of 50 yards on the field using cones or flags. Sprint to the touch line (50 yd.) and return as fast as possible. Repeat this sequence for a total of three trips. The time for completing this run should be in the area between 50 and 65 seconds depending on your fitness level. Your rest-to-work ratio should be 2:1 (if you complete the run in 60 sec., then you should rest for 120 sec. after each run). Perform from 3 to 6 repetitions as you become fit.

300-Yard Shuttle (Short Version)

This is the same as the previous drill, but with a shorter running increment (25 yd.). It will add to the intensity of the run because of the number of touches (stops and starts) in six trips versus three trips. The time to complete the run should be between 55 and 70 seconds, also depending on your conditioning status. Use a rest-to-work ratio of 2:1 (rest twice the amount of time it takes you to complete the run).

5-10-15-20-25 Shuttles

Set markers (cones or flags) every 5 yards from a starting line to total 25 yards on the field. Begin this shuttle run by sprinting to the first marker (5 yd.) out and back. Then go from the start to the second cone and back, start to the third cone and back, and so on. Try to plant and reaccelerate quickly at each successive marker. Complete all five markers in 35 to 45 seconds. Your rest-to-work ratio should be about 3:1 or about 90 seconds per set. Start with 5 repetitions and work up to 10 as your fitness level increases.

1-Minute Sprint Shuttles

Use a designated sprint distance of 25 yards to run out and back continuously for 1 minute. See how much distance you can cover in 1 minute. Try to eliminate pacing the run and instead go as hard as you can for the full minute. Repeat the run after a 3-minute rest. Three to five repetitions in a session would be considered an advanced level.

Fartlek, or Varied-Intensity Conditioning

Fartlek (which means "speed play" in Swedish) training has been around for years. It essentially involves varying the intensity of training. The intensity of the run is changed throughout the workout to extend the conditioning parameters beyond starting levels. This is particularly appropriate for soccer conditioning because of the intermittent nature of the game.

Dribble and Shoot

Position a teammate or coach at the midfield line. Stand at the end line with a ball. Begin by dribbling quickly to the midfield line. As you approach the line, give a short touch pass to your teammate or coach, turn, and begin to sprint back to the starting point, using a bending-type sprint toward the sideline. Your partner will serve a ball out in front of you as you close in on the goal. Control the pass and make a shot on the goal to finish the repetition. Perform 4 repetitions in a set, completing 3 sets. Rest 30 seconds after each repetition and 3 minutes after each set.

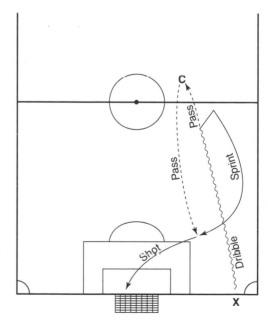

Sprint-Jog-Walk

This drill combines three soccer-related movements. Perform a continuous segment of sprinting (10 sec.), jogging (20 sec.), and walking (10 sec.) for 10 minutes. Include running in curves and angles. Rest 2 minutes and repeat 2 or 3 more sets in the session. Have someone time each segment as you perform the sets.

Sprint-Jog-Backpedal-Curve

Use half the field to sprint half a sideline, jog the end line, backpedal the opposite half sideline, turn at midfield, and run 75 percent around the center circle; do this continuously for 2 minutes. Repeat in the opposite direction. Rest for 2 minutes and repeat. Perform between 3 and 5 sets.

30 On, 30 Off; 15 On, 15 Off

This workout uses the 6-minute run score presented earlier to set a running tempo for conditioning purposes. Because it uses submaximal running intensity (85 percent), this drill is a good way to condition during in-season periods when the legs need to recover from week to week. This should be performed only once a week during the season. Take your 6-minute run distance for 1 minute (e.g., 300 yd./min., which would also represent 100 percent intensity) and divide it in half (150 yd.). This represents the distance needed to be covered in the 30-second work interval. When you reach 30 seconds, reduce the intensity to a 50 percent jog recovery pace or a distance of 75 yards (half of 150 yd.). Use the 30/30 method from 3 to 5 minutes during the season. As you get to peak competition time, you can shorten the work time to 15 seconds, which in the preceding example gives you a working distance of 75 yards and a recovery distance of 37 yards. The main focus here is to complete only the distance prescribed on each run.

Small-Sided Game Conditioning

As mentioned earlier, soccer conditioning should ultimately be training for the game itself. Small-sided games in a confined area will give you game-type conditioning using the actual skills of the game. Although this mode of training requires multiple players, it is well worth the effort to include it in your fitness training. Using indoor facilities (racquetball or basketball courts) will minimize the amount of time spent chasing down errant balls while playing. Keep the playing area reduced to encourage changes of movement. Use from one to five players per team, increasing the playing area as the number of players increases. This mode can be used during both off- and preseason periods to increase your work capacity and sharpen your soccer skills.

1v1

Create a small field (10 yd. by 10 yd.) with goals at each end (cones, field flags, or miniature goals). If you are playing on the field, align a few balls along the perimeter to keep the game moving. Compete for 5 minutes. Play for a total of 4 sets (20 min.) with 90-second rest intervals between sets.

Two In, Five Out

Using the same 10-by-10-yard field, place two players side by side in the center. Five other players arrange themselves around the two middle players. The outside players begin by passing and maneuvering the ball around the inside players with one or two touch passes. The inside players try to steal or stop the passes from continuing within the playing area. If a middle player makes a successful steal or breakup, she switches positions quickly with the player who lost the ball entering the middle, and play continues. Prior to starting, designate the number of passes required to end the game. Increase the intensity by introducing another ball into the game. Along with the conditioning factor, this game builds skill proficiency, reaction time, and agility.

Position-Specific Conditioning

Keeper Combo

This drill is designed specifically for goalkeepers. Position yourself in the center of the mouth of the goal. Start the drill by sprinting to the right corner of the penalty box and touch the ground with your hand. Sprint back quickly to the starting point, touching the ground again. Continue this sequence at both the center point and left corner of the penalty box. After returning from the left corner, complete three vertical jumps in place without stopping. Swing your arms overhead, as if to stop or catch a ball. As you land from the last jump, sprint to the midfield line and rest. Walk back to the starting point as you are resting. Complete 3 repetitions per set for 3 sets. Rest 90 seconds between reps and 3 minutes between sets.

Position Pattern Runs

This conditioning mode specifically conditions players in each position with typical running patterns and maneuvers that occur during the match. Each run uses a prescribed rest interval that may involve soccer skills. This is a good way to peak fitness levels during the preseason and early in-season periods of training.

Use half the field, from sideline to sideline, to mark a variety of running zones designated for each position group. Each position, except for the keeper, begins each sprint at a designated starting marker near midfield. The keeper starts at the mouth of the goal. When completing each run, recover by jogging back to the starting marker. After completing 2 running sets, consisting of 5 runs, take a 5-minute break before finishing 2 more sets. Check your heart rate at the midpoint as well as at the end of the session to determine your work intensity. The run patterns are shown in the diagrams *(a-d)* and described in table 9.2.

Table 9.2 Position Pattern Runs

Position	Run patterns
Forward	1. Crossing run to goal 2. Sideline run 3. Center run to corner (right/left)
Midfielder	1. Sideline run to corner (right/left) 2. Sideline to near post arch run 3. Backpedal 10 yards, turn (right/left), and sprint to far post of goal
Defender	1. Drop-step run to far corner 2. Backpedal 5 yards, turn, and run to top of penalty box 3. Backpedal 10 yards, turn and sprint to far corner of penalty box, turn and sprint back to midfield
Goalkeeper	(*Start the runs at the mouth of the goal) 1. Run from goal to (right/left) sideline 2. Run from goal to center circle 3. Run from goal to (right/left) corner of box, sprint back, repeat to opposite corner, then sprint to center circle

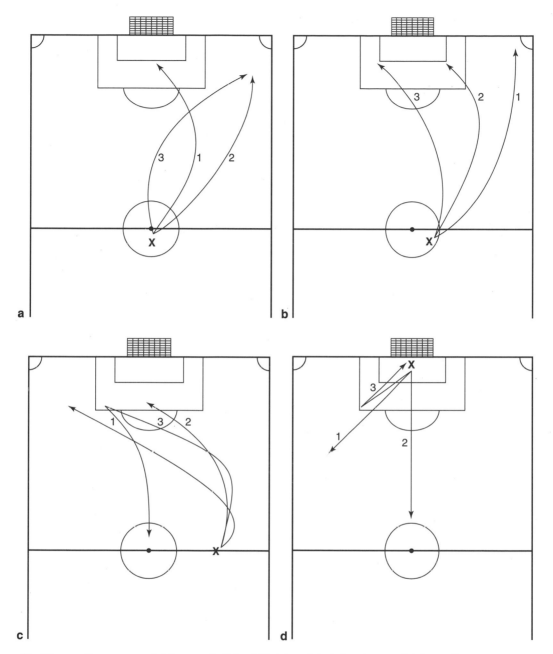

Position pattern runs: *(a)* forward, *(b)* midfielder, *(c)* defender, and *(d)* goalkeeper.

To complete your total soccer fitness program, choose a variety of activities to make use of all of the energy systems required in soccer. Increasing your fitness level can extend your fatigue threshold, helping your performance in the latter part of the match. It can also help you maintain body composition and lessen the chance of injury while under fatigue. Soccer conditioning should involve high-intensity drills to not only maintain the explosive emphasis of the game, but also enable you to work at a high rate for a longer period of time.

Chapter **10**

Match Preparation

O ne of the main goals of a conditioning program for all athletes is to see results that maximize performance on the field. This validation of performance is not always a guarantee. As we have seen, training for soccer athleticism requires proper application, effort, and recovery. This comes to the forefront even more when preparing for competition. The focus during competition shifts to fine-tuning both soccer and basic athletic skills (acceleration, speed, reaction time), while maintaining physical and mental readiness for match play.

Competition schedules vary according to the level of play. Depending on the length of games, they can be played as often as four times a week, sometimes on back-to-back days. Generally speaking, most upper-level players average one or two 90-minute matches a week during big tournament phases. Most high school and college teams maintain a set rhythm so student-athletes can schedule their other responsibilities. To optimize and coordinate training and matches, keep every match as your number one priority, and train for match readiness. Training is still important, but only to prepare for the next competition. Be careful about training during pre- and postmatch days to maintain your energy level for the next performance.

Most of the components we have discussed in previous chapters can, in some form, be trained during match preparation weeks. Be sure, though, to keep in mind your needs and time availability. Heavy training and extra workouts should be replaced by brief sessions designed to heighten and stimulate performance. If you have one match in a 7-day period, the days leading up to the match should be arranged to support match readiness on the scheduled day. Resistance training and conditioning should occur earlier in the week, and drills that heighten the nervous system such as agility and acceleration drills should be performed on the days just prior to game day. Table 10.1 shows a sample training plan for this particular schedule (this reflects only training aspects and not actual practice sessions). Details of this plan are given in the sidebar starting on the following page.

Table 10.1 Sample Training Plan With One Match a Week

Day 1	Day 2	Day 3	Day 4	Day 5	Day 6	Day 7
OFF Recovery	Resistance training (lower-body emphasis)	Conditioning (medium intensity)	Acceleration, agility	Resistance, total body, and power training	Acceleration	MATCH

Designing a training plan can be a little trickier for players who must deal with multiple matches during a 7-day time frame. Because of the intense focus on competition, recovery becomes more of a priority. Resistance training of the lower body may consist of body-weight exercises (squats, lunges, and stretching) along with minimal conditioning (a small set of short sprints, or 3 to 4 min. of 30 on, 30 off runs) following the off day. An additional recovery day is inserted after the first match to prepare for the next match. The remaining days are used for short acceleration and agility training and upper-body strength training. See table 10.2 for a sample schedule.

Table 10.2 Sample Training Plan With Two Matches a Week

Day 1	Day 2	Day 3	Day 4	Day 5	Day 6	Day 7
Resistance training (lower-body emphasis), conditioning	Acceleration, agility	MATCH	Recovery techniques	Resistance, total body, and power training	MATCH	OFF Recovery

MATCH-DAY WARM-UP ROUTINE

As mentioned in chapter 3, activating and stimulating the neuromuscular system during the warm-up will enhance your ability to begin the match in full-speed mode. If your team's warm-up routine doesn't include dynamic stretching, you may want to arrive earlier to the field and perform your own warm-up prior to the team stretch. You can also use dynamic warm-up routines I and II from the flexibility chapter (pages 28 to 30). The routine should take about 10 to 12 minutes from start to finish. Following is a basic active stretching routine that I like to use prematch to build into an acceleration phase that finishes at a full-speed tempo.

TRAINING PLAN AND EMPHASIS
FOR A SINGLE-COMPETITION WEEK

The details of the sample plan shown in table 10.1 are given here.

Day 1. Off day. The day after a match. Use rest and recovery techniques (heat, massage, active rest).

Day 2. Resistance training earlier in the week centers on lower-body exercises and injury prevention. Using low-volume exercises combined with power movements (squats together with squat jumps) is a good way to keep neuromuscular coordination peaking. Strength gains at this point will be minimal; the emphasis is on keeping the body healthy through competition. Injury prevention exercises include single-leg stability drills, joint mobility work, and dynamic hopping or jumping. Keep the volume low to maintain quality. Following are two sample competition-week strength training programs with emphasis on the lower-body and injury prevention. You can choose by location—one program contains exercises to do in a weight room; the other can be done on the field.

Match-Week Resistance Training, Lower-Body Emphasis (Weight Room)

- Single-leg squat with touch to floor, 2 × 3 each leg (touch forward, side, and across)
- Medicine ball lunge and reach (forward), 2 × 5 each leg
- Medicine ball lunge and reach (side), 2 × 5 each leg
- Dumbbell squat to calf raise, 3 × 8
- Squat jump (in place), 2 × 10
- Bench hip bridge, 3 × 8 (with 2 sec. pause)
- Single-leg hop and hold, 3 × 4 each leg (2 × forward/back, 2 × side to side), hold 2 seconds

Resistance Training, Lower-Body Emphasis (Field Alternative)

- Single-leg squat with touch to ground, 2 × 3 each leg (touch forward, side, and across)
- Lunge and reach (forward), 2 × 6 each leg
- Lunge and reach (side), 2 × 6 each leg
- Body-weight squat to calf raise, 3 × 6 combined with squat jump × 5 (perform 6 repetitions of the squat to calf raise, then finish the set with 5 squat jumps; do 3 sets)
- Lying hip bridges (two feet), 2 × 10, hold 2 seconds
- Single-leg hops with hold (forward), 2 × 4 each leg, hold 2 seconds

(continued)

Day 3. Conditioning early in the week to enhance anaerobic energy and overall fitness during the season. This conditioning period does not require heavy volume (repetitions) or long durations to be effective. It should be an extension of practice time and complement the week's overall plan. See the following details.

Conditioning Session

- Run 5 × 60 yards at 80 percent (25 sec. rests between sets)
- 2-minute rest
- 2 × 3-minute run, distance based on 6-minute run score (use perimeter of field) at 75 percent (3 min. rest between sets)
- Stretch recovery

Day 4. Acceleration and agility emphasis. Two or three days before match day is a good time to incorporate short, quick, explosive acceleration or agility-type drills. Distances of 10 to 20 yards are sufficient to stimulate the neuromuscular system for match readiness. The volume should stay low to maintain the appropriate intensity, which can deteriorate when you become fatigued.

Combined Agility and Acceleration Workout (Before Practice)

Designate a 20-yard distance with markers. Place a short half-speed ladder (five spaces) or four soccer discs in a line on the ground at the beginning of the drill distance. Start by performing a quick footwork pattern through the ladder or cones and then accelerate full speed past the last marker. After slowing down, return to the starting position while jogging at 50 percent effort. Attempt to finish 4 repetitions in 30 seconds. Rest 30 seconds, and repeat for 4 to 6 sets. Use the following footwork patterns as a guideline for the agility part of each set:

- Alternating two steps forward
- Alternating two steps lateral
- Diagonal shuffle forward
- Diagonal shuffle backward
- Two-foot quick hops, forward and lateral

Day 5. Resistance, total-body, and power training. The second resistance training session consists of total-body movements that combine upper-body and lower-body exercises for condensing total workout time. Power exercises are also a good way to activate and excite the neuromuscular system for the match to shortly follow. Two options are given here—one for in the weight room and one for on the field.

Total-Body Resistance and Power Training (Weight Room)

- Dumbbell high pull, 3 × 6
- Dumbbell squat to curl and press, 2 × 6
- Dumbbell jump shrug, 3 × 6

- Medicine ball squat and throw, 3 × 4
- Plyometric combo: Alternating split jumps × 4 each, lateral bounds (ice skaters) × 8 each, squat jump × 5
- Core training: Medicine ball lying pullover throw (wall) × 10, medicine ball seated twists × 20, lying leg raises × 20

Total-Body Resistance and Power Training (Field Alternative)

- *Stations set on field area:* 20 seconds of work, 40 seconds of rest, one or two cycles with a partner
- Station 1: Lying pullover throw to partner (use soccer ball and accelerate the ball quickly)
- Station 2: Power push-up (attempt to get off the ground with each repetition)
- Station 3: Alternating split jumps
- Station 4: Lateral bounds (ice skaters)
- Station 5: Speed ladder alternating diagonal bounds (forward and backward)
- Station 6: Lying leg raises to 90 degrees (partner stands behind and throws legs to the ground)

Day 6. Acceleration. The day before a match is a good day to perform a quick acceleration session at either the beginning or end of practice to give a final kick to prime the body for competition. This should be the final training preparation for the week. This session should be intense, but not high volume.

Acceleration Session (Day Before the Match)

Use a 20-yard area and perform the following sequence of movements at full speed:

- Lean, fall, and go × 2
- Ankle bounce (in place) to acceleration × 2
- Side shuffle (three steps) to acceleration × 2
- Diagonal shuffle (forward), plant and go × 2
- Diagonal shuffle (backward), turn and go × 2
- Alternating diagonal bound × 4 to acceleration × 2
- Squat jumps (in place), 2 × 10 (1 min. rest between sets)

Day 7. Match play. This is the ultimate test. This is why you train. Everything to this point is to help your performance in the match. You should have a routine and plan for match day for preparing for, participating in, and recovering from the match. Specifics such as rest, nutrition, and hydration (discussed in chapter 11) should be addressed in addition to the week's training. See pages 148 to 151 for some match-day techniques to consider before, during, and after the match.

Prematch Warm-Up

Use a 20- to 25-yard marked distance with the halfway point marked (10 to 12 yd.). I like using the area from one sideline across the field to about the middle of the center circle. Use the movements and stretches listed in the following table.

To the middle of the field	On return back from the middle of the field
Jog to the middle of the circle	Backpedal to the sideline
Alternating hamstring (hands on hips, front toe up)	Side shuffle (stand tall, arms swing overhead)
Hip sit stretch (cross one leg over the lap and sit back)	Carioca (cross knee over high)
Walking knee hug to lunge and twist (pull knee high, step out long, and twist to front leg)	Open and close hip rotation (knee high, rotate leg in or out)
Alternating hip stretch (elbow inside front leg, push back to hamstring hold)	Skip with extension (of lower leg)
Leg swing (stand tall, swing leg to opposite hand)	Backward run (long reach, use arms)
Side lunge (sit on lead foot, trail leg straight, feet flat, hands inside feet)	Side skip (front leg reaches, back leg pushes)
Quadriceps stretch (pull foot behind with two hands and hold)	High knee running to heel kicks

At this point, the warm-up should increase in tempo to end with a few full-speed bursts. Use the first half of the area to accelerate through and the second half as a slow-down zone. After slowing down, turn around and jog back to the start at 50 percent of your maximum speed. Use the following combinations of footwork, hops, and jumps before each acceleration run:

Jog halfway and then sprint (75% speed)

Alternate fast feet in place for 5 yards and then sprint (75%)

Alternate scissor steps in place and then sprint (75%)

Side shuffle (right and left), turn and sprint (85%)

Diagonal shuffle step (right and left diagonal cutting) 5 yards and then sprint (85%)

Drop-step shuffle backward (right and left) 5 yards; turn and sprint (85%)

Simulated header (jump up) and then sprint (95%)

Shuttle sprint (5 yd. out, 5 yd. back), turn again and sprint (100%)

Tuck jumps (jump up attempting to bring the knees to the chest) × 2 and then sprint (100%)

WARM-UP FOR ALTERNATES IN THE GAME

After the initial warm-up, match play should begin within a few minutes. However, only 11 players can be on the field at once. If you are on the bench as an alternate or substitute player, you have the challenge of having to bring your body to a readiness state at a moment's notice. Typically, you will have only a few minutes to get ready for full-speed play. In this situation I suggest a scaled-back version of the previous warm-up that targets and stimulates the main areas. Here is a sample of this type of mini-warm-up:

Alternate's Warm-Up

Use a 10- to 15-yard area behind the bench.

Jog down and backpedal back

Skip down with the arms crossing in and out and backward skip back

Marching leg swings down and alternating single toe touch back

Alternating side lunges down and side skips back

Alternating quad stretch hold down and heel kick back

At this point, begin moving with increased tempo to excite the neuromuscular system. Use the same distance as in the previous movements, gradually increasing the intensity level as in the pregame warm-up so that the last few repetitions are at full speed.

Side shuffle down and carioca back

Ankle bounce in place (2 sec.) and then sprint 10 yards (75%)

Backpedal 6 steps, turn and sprint 10 yards (85%)

Simulated header in place, turn and sprint 10 yards (95%)

Two tuck jumps (knees to chest) in place, turn and sprint 10 yards (100%)

©Human Kinetics

Good match-week planning, including warm-ups and cool-downs, will help keep you fresh and ready to play at your best.

STARTING UP AFTER HALFTIME

Another period of time to consider when dealing with match readiness is halftime, during which you can be resting anywhere from 20 to 30 minutes. With this amount of inactive time, you should consider a second restart to prepare for another 45-minute match. This can also be a time to use the ball in movement drills. Lean toward synchronizing the whole body into readiness for the second half using short, quick, and explosive movements as you finish this segment.

Post-Halftime Warm-Up

Move around in no particular direction, performing each combination for about 20 seconds. Use the ball either solo or with a partner as listed.

Shuffle and carioca

Skip and backpedal

High knee running and backward running

Heel kicks and power skips

Cut and move (diagonal cutting, moving forward) and diagonal backward shuffle (defensive marking)

Two minutes of dribbling and touch passing with a partner

Pass and accelerate (with partner) for 10 yards × 4 (85%)

Receive pass, control, pass back, and accelerate (with partner) × 4 (95%)

Tuck jumps × 2 and accelerate for 10 yards (100%)

COOLING DOWN AFTER THE MATCH

When the final whistle sounds and competition ends, consideration should be given to a cooling-down process. A minimal amount of flexibility and recovery work will help with gradually bringing you back to a normal relaxed state. Depending on the amount of actual playing time you've had, as little as 5 minutes can help alleviate the stresses of competition. Light jogging and stretching (some dynamic and mostly static) is recommended as a general cool-down routine. Away from the field, incorporate the self-massage, foam rolling, and warm bath techniques discussed in chapter 11.

Five-Minute Postmatch Cool-Down Routine

Easy jog around the perimeter of the field

Walking toe touches × 5, hold each stretch for 10 seconds

Sumo squat stretch (push knees out with elbows), hold for 10 seconds

Lateral (side) lunge (hands inside the feet), hold for 10 seconds each side

Kneeling hip flexor (arms reaching overhead), hold for 10 seconds each leg

Standing leg swings (forward and back, out to the side, and rotational forward and back) × 5 each leg, each direction

Body check stretch—perform any stretch you feel needs extra attention

To bring your performance level to a peak for competition, develop a game-week training plan. The plan should have the proper training volume and loads leading up to the match. Match preparation training should center on high-intensity, short-duration drills that excite the body to increase readiness as well as help with recovery from practice sessions. After competition, restore balance by performing a proper cool-down to prepare for future competition.

Chapter 11

Recovery and Injury Prevention

Stress on the human body can manifest in many forms. For the athlete, prolonged physical and mental stress from the rigors of training and competition can compound into a performance plateau or chronic injury. This is why you must incorporate planned breaks and recovery techniques into your overall training plan. When your training becomes more intense and advanced, recovery becomes as important as the training itself. The value of regeneration can't be overstated. It can be as simple as a day completely off from training or getting the correct amount of sleep. As you become more involved and begin to specialize in your sport, you may adopt the belief, as many developing athletes do, that if your training is working, doing more will be even better. This leads to becoming overworked and fatigued. This chapter discusses techniques to lessen the chance of overtraining, describes the recovery process, and explores ways to reduce injuries in the training process.

For years, soccer players gained fitness by playing the game. Many coaches used the preseason to condition players using simulated match play. The belief was that the more practice matches they played prior to the full season, the better players' fitness levels would be. This seems to be the mind-set in many of today's youth soccer programs. It's not uncommon for players of all ages to compete in 40 to 50 matches a year. This type of volume creates two problems: (1) The athlete gets fatigued, burned out, or injured, and (2) time and energy are taken away from normal physical athletic development and regeneration for the next competitive season. These players are locked into a competition mode that can become hazardous to the body, especially if they are young and developing. Although today's coaches and players are in general more knowledgeable about the importance of physical and mental stress maintenance, there still seems to be an overwhelming amount of competition at all levels of soccer play. Managing the highs and lows of your training and competition will allow for a more natural progression of improvement and success.

HEALTHY RECOVERY

To stay balanced, the body is constantly resisting and adapting to stress. Stress is all around us—from the weather, to school or work, to the common cold. Training and competition are no different. All training is stressful in the sense that it challenges your body's normal levels. Regardless of the cause, the body can adapt to stress in either a positive or negative way. At the beginning of a training cycle, most likely coming off a season-ending recovery period, your body will have an alarming reaction that disrupts its balance. If you have ever experienced working out after a long layoff, you know how this feels. Muscles get sore, and your energy is zapped quickly. As the training load gradually continues, your body learns to compensate and adapt to a higher level that can be challenged again. This is the ideal training environment. This can also be the toughest part of designing your program: knowing when to increase volume or intensity and when not to.

©Scott Bales/Icon SMI

To develop a sound training plan, you must distinguish between volume (how much) and intensity (how hard). If you want to perform a tough workout that is very intense, then you need to moderate the amount of work (volume). The reverse is also true; you can increase one (intensity or volume), but not both.

The demands of the game require recovery strategies to keep you healthy and get you ready for the next match.

Increasing both will ultimately cause your improvement to level off or diminish. Make sound decisions about your training plan. Doing more isn't always the right answer.

Recovering After a Match or Workout

To produce quality effort for each match or workout, you must adjust your intensity level during the days following a competition or workout and leading up to the next session. At the peak of the playing schedule, you should have a "less is more" approach to training and workouts to deliver the proper amount of stimulus for maintaining performance levels. Spiking the effect of training during this time requires smaller amounts that will keep you feeling ready for upcoming contests.

Depending on the number of minutes played, your body can be fatigued, stiff, and sore from a match or workout. A recovery workout the next day will help dissipate these symptoms as well as help you regain normal levels of function. These recovery sessions don't need to be too extensive (15 to 30 min.), but they should be performed with the goal of counteracting the stress that occurred during competition.

The most common recovery after competition is the postmatch cooldown. This is a way to gradually slow your body down while keeping your blood moving through your muscles. Most cool-downs consist of light movement drills such as shuffling, skipping, and carioca, combined with static stretching. Once you leave the field and get home or to the locker room, the combination of submerging your body in a cool bath and taking a hot shower or warm bath can help to speed the recovery process.

To lessen training stress, plan recovery sessions to be used during, after, and between workouts. Long-term training with adjusted intensity and volume without periods of recovery can lead to decreased performance and unnecessary fatigue. Each phase of your workouts should transition to the next by reducing the level of workout intensity. In this way you will be able to regenerate before increasing your workload. Usually, this transition period lasts about a week. Heavy training days should be followed by a lighter training day or rest to keep the training pattern wavelike, with bouts of high, medium, and low levels of work to help build back readiness for the next heavy training session. Training sessions should also end with a general cool-down period in which light movement, stretching, and self-massage (discussed later in this chapter) are used to alleviate the soreness associated with the breakdown of the body.

Preventing Overtraining

The following signals may signify overtraining:

- Lack of motivation to train and compete
- Constant fatigue

- Chronic muscle tightness or soreness
- Decreased performance
- Chronic injuries (mostly muscle pulls or strains) that won't go away
- Susceptibility to sickness and colds

Overtraining as a result of too much intensity or volume during workouts will lead to the breakdown and loss of positive training results. An effective training plan is based on your training experience and the demands of other activities (practice, games). To reduce overtraining, study your competition schedule. Identify times when you know you will need a rest or recovery period. This should reveal the amount of time, in terms of weeks and days, that you have for training between competitive and noncompetitive seasons. If the time you have for training is limited, which is quite likely, then search for smaller periods of time in which to insert even a limited amount of maintenance work, such as a week during the season when you are playing a weaker opponent, or a few weeks during the transition from school to club seasons. The key is to be creative in finding time that doesn't become excessive or take away the effect of actually performing some training.

Overtraining can cause your performance and improvement level to stalemate or decrease even with a good training background. Another physical condition that can occur when initiating a new program or ramping up a current program is delayed-onset muscle soreness, or DOMS.

This delayed soreness can last from 2 to 7 days with the second day postexercise typically being the worst day. One theory is that during exercise small microtears occur in the muscles being worked. The muscles respond through stiffness and soreness almost to the point of pain, which can last for multiple days. This discomfort indicates that the muscles are beginning the process of recovery. Usually, light stretching and contrast-type (hot and cold) therapy can help to treat this condition. Staying conscious of your current fitness level and trying not to overdo training volume or intensity will also help to keep soreness manageable.

It is also important to mention that proper rest, nutrition, and hydration will create the right environment for positive training. Many young athletes lose sight of the fact that the body's adaptive response to training is occurring while at rest. The growth and repair during the recovery process is an important part of the training equation.

By learning how much training, playing stress, and practice your body can respond to, you can design a program to fit your schedule without fear of overextending yourself. As mentioned earlier, one way to initiate this is to classify your workouts as light, medium, hard, or very hard. Light would be considered a recovery-type workout that prepares your body for the next day's training and allows for active recovery following a heavy training day or match. A medium day would involve an increase of intensity that still gives you the ability to train the next day without any side effects. The hard category kicks up the intensity once again, but to the point that a recovery day may be needed. A very hard session would warrant multiple days before undertaking another one of the same degree. Following is a list of exercises classified by effort, or intensity.

Exercise	Effort classification
Combination jog or stride, 20 minutes	Light
10 × 100 meters @ 75% with recovery	Medium
7 × 300-yard shuttle runs @ 60 seconds	Hard
6 × 50-yard hill sprints, 4 × 50-yard alternating bounds, and 5-minute run for distance	Very hard

As you get into the competitive season, your training volume should be reduced, and focus should shift from fitness to fine-tuning technique and soccer-specific work. The next section outlines additional ways to combat training stress.

Additional Recovery Techniques

As mentioned previously, creating the right training environment should also include arranging aspects of the posttraining period away from the training place. The inclusion of proper diet, hydration, and preventive injury and recovery techniques will give you synergistic results that are positive to the whole training process. Let's explore some of the basic areas.

Nutrition

The foods you eat are the fuel for your body. Just as a high-performance sports car needs good fuel, an athlete requires high-quality nutrition. This is a critical part of recovery when attempting to perform at a high level. It is important to maintain a balance of the basic food nutrients (carbohydrate, fat, and protein); carbohydrate should be the primary energy source. Stored glucose (glycogen) must be replenished through the intake of carbohydrate before, during (usually through sport drinks), and after practice or competition. It should total around 55 to 60 percent of your total calories for the day. Choose good carbohydrate from starches (pasta, potatoes, rice, and breads), fruits and vegetables, and dairy products (which provide calcium to restore the body).

A misconception among many athletes is that they should consume an excessive amount of protein when they are competing. In fact, protein needs range from 1 to 3 grams per kilogram of body weight (1 kg = 2.2 lb.).

Athletes in high-intensity training require more protein than normal because of the increased workload. Be aware that the body can digest only about 35 to 50 grams of protein effectively at any one time; anything in addition to that amount is eliminated with no benefit derived. During recovery, protein is used for building, maintaining, and repairing muscle broken down during exercise. Neglecting protein can cause a loss in bone and soft-tissue integrity leading to strains, pulls, stress fractures, and other chronic breakdowns of the body.

Use the 3:2:1 ratio to determine how many calories should come from carbohydrate, protein, and fat throughout the day. You should consume three times the amount of calories in the form of carbohydrate than fat and twice the amount of calories from protein than fat. This method helps to keep fat intake low while maintaining the proper intake of carbohydrate and protein.

Fat intake for athletes should be less than 80 grams each day, or 18 percent of the total caloric intake. Not all fats are bad. Saturated fat and cholesterol can lead to cardiovascular disease, but monounsaturated and polyunsaturated fats are necessary for cellular function and other body processes.

To balance your caloric intake with your training output, you need to eat more than you may think. Taking in less can cause a drop in body weight that will lower your overall muscle mass, which can affect performance. What should your total caloric intake be? Although every person is unique, elite athletes can require up to 4,000 calories a day. The following formulas can help you estimate your caloric needs:

Male athletes: 42-50 kcal/kg body weight/day (depending on your activity)

Female athletes: 30-35 kcal/kg body weight/day (depending on your activity)

The higher your training intensity is, the higher your caloric needs will be. Your weight in pounds divided by 2.2 is your weight in kilograms. For example, a 150-pound male player would use this calculation:

150 lb. / 2.2 = 68.2 kg

68.2 kg $\times$ 42 kcal/day = 2,864.4 kcal/day

This athlete needs to eat about 2,864 calories each day to keep his body weight at 150 pounds. If he wants to gain muscle mass, then he must eat more food. This food intake must be quality food eaten throughout the day and not just at one meal.

Along with the three basic nutrients, all athletes should also ingest key vitamins and minerals to manage training stress. Vitamins are organic compounds needed for normal growth and repair. They also play a part in energy reactions including cellular maintenance, healing, and fighting infection. Vitamins E, A, and C are the most necessary. Minerals are the compounds that the body requires to start many of the metabolic reactions including the transport of oxygen to the muscle, the breakdown of energy ATP, and the transport of nerve impulses. Athletes need iron, zinc, magnesium, and calcium.

You may want to consult a nutritional professional for advice on proper athletic nutrition. You'll notice the difference on the field!

Hydration

Maintaining fluid levels before, during, and after training and competition will aid in muscle contraction and heat dissipation, as well as other bodily functions. Most athletes are conscious of the need to hydrate only when they become thirsty, but this is usually too late. Soccer doesn't lend itself to many breaks other than halftime, when good hydration can take place. This is why it is important prior to competition to increase body fluid levels. One of the easiest indicators of a need for hydrating is urine color. A dark and concentrated color indicates dehydration. Using water and drinks with electrolytes will have a positive effect on maintaining your levels, especially during cooler weather when thirst may be less noticeable.

You should consume fluids and carbohydrate immediately after exercise to replace the fluid lost in sweat and to replenish muscle glycogen reserves. You need to replace both water and electrolytes to keep from becoming dehydrated and cramping. Recovery drinks such as Gatorade help replace salts lost in sweat and can be a better choice on hot and humid days. Fruits and raw vegetables can also be wise choices for pre- and postmatch snacks because they can also supply extra hydration as a result of their water content. You may be surprised at how proper hydration directly affects your performance.

Quality Sleep

Your body uses rest time to repair itself from training stress. What is mistakenly referred to as the "building up process" (conditioning, weight training, speed development) is actually time spent tearing down the body. At rest your body can adapt and repair to prepare for more training down the road. Try to establish normal sleeping patterns and conditions that will create a quality sleep mode. A dark and quiet sleeping area, comfortable sleep clothing, and a comfortable temperature will help you recover from the stresses of training, practice, and competition. Most experts recommend around 8 hours of sleep per night. This can be a starting point that can be adjusted based on individual needs. The key is to understand your body's natural rhythm and be consistent.

Massage

Massage therapy has always been popular with athletes as a recovery technique. The deep tissuc technique is a good way to help speed up recovery from tissue breakdown by manipulating overused muscle and other soft tissues (tendons, ligaments) through touch pressure. The kneading action of massage can increase blood flow and help move the waste products from exercise out of the muscle quicker. Professional massages can, however, be expensive. An alternative is to use a foam roller to simulate massage care (figure 11.1, *a-c*). This technique uses body weight and gravity to produce the same effect as massage. Use the rolling action of the tube to work up and down the length of the targeted muscle. If any area of the muscle is tender as you roll, hold the spot for a few seconds and then continue to any other areas in need of attention. This technique can also help activate and stimulate nerve endings in the muscle as part of a warm-up session.

Figure 11.1   Using a foam roller for massage on *(a)* hamstrings, *(b)* glutes, and *(c)* hips.

Hot and Cold Contrast Baths

Taking alternating hot and cold baths is a good way to cause a natural "milking effect" throughout the blood vessels in the designated area. Heat opens blood vessels and cold constricts them. This opening and closing action dissipates the waste products of exercise. Cold temperature on its own is better used immediately after training or competition, to calm the body down. Use about 5 minutes for heat and around a minute for the cold aspect of this recovery method.

Getting yourself in a balanced state after training or competition takes concentrated effort. However, being consistent with basic rest, nutrition, and hydration is a good start toward regeneration and will pay high dividends in the day-to-day maintenance of your personal fitness level. Planning and controlling your workouts and fueling and hydrating your body also have a secondary effect of helping control injury rates. If you are fatigued, lacking nutrients and minerals, or dehydrated, chances are your performance is suffering. You will begin to have trouble bouncing back from minor injuries that turn into chronic problems (strains, pulls). Remember, training is only half the solution. What you do after training can also affect your performance.

INJURY PREVENTION

No matter how much you prepare for the game, injuries are inevitable. Soccer is a contact sport, and your body will be challenged regularly as you compete. Most soccer injuries occur to soft tissue. It is not uncommon to see bumps, bruises, and even concussions in soccer games. Strains, pulls, and tears to ligaments and muscles materialize because of the twisting, turning, and high-velocity nature of the game. In fact, torn knee ligaments (especially the anterior cruciate ligament, or ACL) are common among female players; some are the result of limited preparation.

Although the majority of injuries come with the territory, taking preventive measures to limit injuries will help keep you on the field. You are already aware that a consistent flexibility and strength training routine can help protect you from injuries. Keeping specific muscle groups such as hip flexors, hamstrings, calves, and the lower back flexible will cut down on strains and pulls that can develop during a long season. Good nutrition, adequate rest, and other recovery methods will also help to minimize soccer-related injuries.

ACL Injury

The ligaments surrounding the knee joint, like all ligaments of the body, provide structure and stability whether you are stationary or in motion. These ligaments are interlaced in and around the knee from all directions to support high-velocity movements (running, cutting, jumping). The knee is classified as a hinge joint that, like a door, bends and extends the lower leg forward and backward. The degree of movement that can occur sideways and rotationally is limited.

The reactive play during a soccer match can sometimes put the knees in compromising positions. These positions can be risky if the musculature around the knees (hamstrings, quadriceps, calves, and groin) is underdeveloped or weak from a previous injury. Even though female players tend to have a higher ACL injury rate than male players do, it should be a concern for all soccer players, especially those who lack extensive training experience. Research tells us that these rates increase because of several factors, some controllable and others not. Differences in muscle firing patterns, hip angles, muscle balance, and even hormones have all been linked to ACL problems. Although no one is quite sure why these occurrences are more prevalent in female athletes, it's been my experience that muscle imbalances and lack of training the legs at high speeds and in multiple directions seem to be key factors in driving these injuries.

A preventive focus can become part of your warm-up, conditioning, or postpractice routine. Strength work should focus on the front, side, and back of the knee as well as anterior, posterior, and rotational movement patterns to completely develop all functional aspects of the leg. Exercises such as multidirectional lunges, step-ups, and jumps strengthen the joint in a controlled environment, whereas performing active stability (balance) drills, such as those presented in chapter 4, target the knee in all three planes of motion and provide dynamic strength to the ankle, knee, and hip, creating a solid structure during high-velocity movement. Following is a sample drill menu geared to prepare and maintain sound structure around the knee for injury protection.

Medicine ball single-leg squat and reach, 2 × 10 each leg

Lateral lunge (body weight), 2 × 10 each side

Medicine ball single-leg Romanian deadlift, 2 × 10 each leg

Rotational lunge (body weight), 2 × 10 each leg

Single-leg hop and hold (front-side-turn), 2 × 3 each way

Two-foot 180-degree jump (jump off two feet, land on one),
   1 × 5 each leg

This sequence can be used pre- or postpractice as well as before a strength training session once or twice per week, depending on your period of training.

Muscle Strains and Pulls

Other common mishaps on the soccer field are muscle strains and pulls. In soccer the majority of these injuries occur in the lower body. The kicking, sprinting, cutting, backpedaling, and jumping that are regularly part of the game can take their toll on the body during the course of a long season. Adding a fatigue factor from extensive play periods can also cause running technique and core strength to break down and increase the chance of straining or pulling. Lack of or limited warm-up periods can set up a situation in which you are not ready for full-speed performance.

Strained or pulled hamstrings, groins, and hip flexors tend to draw the most attention for soccer players.

To minimize these injuries, use a solid warm-up period, but also train these muscle groups through a full range of motion using ground-based positions (on your feet) to develop movement patterns that will transfer to the field. Sitting in a machine does not transfer well to the field and thus is less than appropriate for soccer players. Preventive exercises include the step-up (18 to 21 in., or 45 to 53 cm), the single-leg Romanian deadlift using a dumbbell, front and side lunges, and even stepping over adjustable hurdles at various heights. Performing 2 sets of 10 to 12 repetitions should provide the stimulus needed to improve muscle length and coordination for a carryover effect.

Concussions

Because of the contact nature of soccer, concussions are common. A concussion is an injury to the brain caused by trauma to the head. Collisions in the air through set pieces or attempting to head a 50/50 ball with a competitor can result in a blow from someone's head, arm, or leg, resulting in a concussion. Concussions can be hard to diagnose. Some signs to look for are headaches, dizziness, confusion, memory loss, loss of balance, and nausea. Severe concussions require medical attention from a licensed physician and may result in your having to have complete rest from competition and practice until rechecked. As with any accident, it is important to follow the recovery instructions and be patient with your progress. Trying to come back too early can worsen the situation and possibly prevent any chance of playing again.

Reaching peak performance without breaking down requires good management of the stress from training and competition. Use nutrition, rest, and hydration to restore your body and prevent injury while you adapt to new levels of training. Using an ACL preventive routine will increase the integrity of your ankles, knees, and hips and develop the structural strength required for soccer. Knowing that injuries can sometimes be unavoidable, try to minimize their effect on your performance by using the preventive measures discussed here.

Chapter 12

Year-Round Training Plans

Now that you have a basic understanding of the training components and other factors to consider to improve your soccer performance, the next question is *How do you put this information together to create a plan that will give you the results you're looking for?* This is not always an easy task. Program design is a combination of art and science; in other words, it is based on scientific principles and creative intuition. When designing your program, you need to consider the energy systems to emphasize while conditioning, when to strength train during the competitive season, and how to peak power for transfer on the field. Your plan should be balanced, challenging, and motivating while fitting the style and play of your team. It should also have purpose and direction; otherwise, it can become a hodgepodge of meaningless work. This final chapter is devoted to developing a training template for organizing your individual and specific soccer conditioning plan.

TRAINING WITH PERIODIZATION

Traditionally, a yearly training program is divided into sections, or phases, to address the various training components. This method is also known as periodization. By defining phases of the training year, you can control new stimulus to raise your training level for the next phase. This can help you to avoid overtraining or a negative training effect. Periodizing your program in a progressive manner will also keep you from leveling off, or reaching a plateau of adaptation.

The athlete's overall training period is called a macrocycle. The macrocycle may be longer than a year (as is the case with Olympic athletes, who can have 4-year macrocycles) and culminates in the competitions with the most priority (major matches or championship matches). The macrocycle is broken down into several mesocycles that are anywhere from 4 to 6 weeks in length and involve specific training phases. Each phase has specific training variables including frequency, duration, intensity, and load. An example of this is a transition phase geared to regenerating the body after a long competitive season. Each new phase builds from the previous one, with all phases directed to the overall objectives. These phases are then broken down into microcycles consisting of a training week (or weeks). The microcycle addresses the day-to-day specifics for that particular training week including exercises, repetition and set quantities, rest intervals, tempo, and so forth. This is also the level at which workout plans can be adjusted based on observed changes. Using this general format, the following phases of the soccer player's training year are designated throughout this chapter:

- **Transition phase.** This is the period between the final competition of the year and the start of a noncompetitive cycle of training. Some macrocycles include multiple transition phases, some of which are between other phases to facilitate recovery without a long period of downtime. Typically, recovery from the season will have high priority during this phase and involve active rest or cross-training techniques without complete rest. Active rest refers to gradually reducing the amount of training stress by performing low-level activity. Your body will respond to the next training cycle more easily if you maintain general fitness while simultaneously allowing for mental recovery from previous training. For a soccer player, the transition phase may include activities such as swimming, biking, or even tennis to change the normal training routine. The frequency, duration, and intensity will all be at the lower end of the training spectrum. This phase can last from 1 to 2 weeks.

- **Preparation phase.** This is the phase in which the bulk of off-season training will occur. This phase is usually designed as two parts—general and specific. The purpose of the first part is to develop the work capacity lost during competition. Workouts are designed to stress the body for adaptation. The second part is designed to reacquire the motor patterns and skills related to soccer. An important goal of the preparation phase is to build back the strength and speed that are compromised during the competitive season. Although some soccer skill work may be performed during this phase, the emphasis should be on developing your physical qualities. Each part can last from 4 to 6 weeks, and then you dovetail into the precompetition phase.

- **Precompetition phase.** During the precompetition phase, brief but intense work is used to prime the body for the upcoming season. This can also serve as a period in which to peak performance for carryover into the early season. Practice time is now part of the training equation, and recovery for both practice and training becomes an important variable. This is usually a shorter phase (2 or 3 weeks), or it can be an extension of the preparation phase, in which the last few weeks emphasize peak training. Training volume should drop during this phase to increase recovery, and all training is geared toward readiness for match play.

• **Competition phase.** The competition phase can be broken down into early season, midseason, late season, and championship season. Priority during this phase is to maintain as much of the physical qualities gained during the off-season as possible to lessen the chance of detraining. Detraining refers to the total loss of the training effect gained during the normal conditioning process. By reducing the fitness training too long, most of the training benefits will be lost during the season. The training volume will be low and brief, but workouts will continue to be of high quality and intense. Injury prevention should also be a focus of this phase, using pre- or postworkout or practice preventive exercises to maintain physical integrity during the season. Typically, any workouts during this phase are based on when the next match is without losing continuity by going too long between sessions. Usually, the most demanding workout is performed earlier in the week, and workouts closer to competition consist of neuromuscular activation (short, explosive, power based) for match readiness.

Using a classic periodization approach in a soccer conditioning program involves some challenges. One is the fact that most soccer players today have extended or multiple competitive seasons. Specialization in one sport is starting at an earlier age than ever before, and it is not uncommon to see young soccer players playing 30 to 40 matches per year. This leaves little or no time to regenerate from the previous season, and limits the time available to develop any fitness components for the following season.

Another problem is that young players are less active than players were in the past. Less activity means less natural development of the basic movement skills needed for improved performance. Their soccer skills are very polished, but their basic movement skills are lacking. For these reasons, many young players do not develop with any consistency or progression, resulting in their not reaching their performance potential. They are also increasingly susceptible to chronic injuries that can further hinder development.

This doesn't mean that physical training is impossible, but rather that creativity is needed to create a consistent training plan. You may have to stay in a competition phase longer and then increase the intensity of training when you have minibreaks throughout the season. Even though doing so may shorten the training time and lessen the training effect, a small commitment to training will help in your overall development as a player.

CONSTRUCTING A TRAINING PLAN

This section offers a step-by-step approach to designing your training program. Remember that program design involves some creative measures, so don't believe there is only one way to create an individual plan. Use this outline in conjunction with your personal schedule to develop the best possible system.

1. Configure the time available to train from your yearly schedule by first listing the major matches or tournaments for the year. By not listing some of the less competitive matches, you can continue to train without having to work peaking or extra rest into the phase.

2. From this available time, insert planned recovery and rest periods. This should include the time frame in which you want to peak the training before competition as well as holidays and school exam periods. Transition phases that involve active rest or cross-training should be considered planned recovery. For young players there should be an extended recovery time in which to cross-train with non-soccer-related activities that will help regenerate enthusiasm for the next season.

3. Work backward from the rest periods and place the training time into phases based on transition (active rest), preparation, precompetition, and competition seasons. Remember that you don't have to use all the phases. Use training phases that are at least 4 weeks long to ensure that you have enough training time for your body to adapt. If you are unable to find 4 consecutive weeks, use the time available in a sensible manner. Two-week blocks of time are better than none. The key is to train with a purpose at each workout.

4. Develop training goals and a needs list based on initial or current baseline testing or evaluation. If you've never tested your athleticism before, refer to chapter 2 for appropriate tests. Consider your training age and experience when you prepare a plan of attack. For example, if you are lacking training experience, spend the majority of your training time developing basic athletic skills through a longer non-competition phase. Athletic skills such as balance, coordination, and strength need to be addressed before advancing to specific training (kicking power or jumping height). This will ensure that you have a solid base that you can transfer later to higher training levels and activities displayed on the field.

5. Incorporate a training theme during each phase that will give your training a purpose and reflect your goals. Themes such as developing general strength and acceleration, increasing explosive power, and raising anaerobic conditioning levels will give direction to your phases and help you to address your individual needs.

6. Depending on the phase or theme you establish, develop an exercise list for resistance training, balance and flexibility training, agility and speed training, and conditioning that will drive the program during each workout. This again should be based on your needs and not a barrage of unnecessary drills. Consider quality over quantity when deciding. It's nice to be thorough, but your training time may be limited, and you don't want to waste energy. Classify the resistance exercises into manageable groups using upper-body emphasis, lower-body emphasis, core strengthening, or total-body power.

7. Structure your daily plans with exercises from your menu. Train each fitness component according to the number of days you are training. Train each component no more than three times a week, and change exercises every so often to eliminate staleness.

8. Implement the plan.

9. Evaluate your progress following long training phases or before the competitive season to see whether you need to adjust the program. An evaluation can be as simple as the 10-yard acceleration or incline pull-up repetition test. Tweak weekly plans with this snapshot information.

ORGANIZING TRAINING WITH ATHLETIC DEVELOPMENT

A good way to make certain that your training not only is appropriate but also increases your athletic development level is to recognize your stage of maturation and potential. I often receive requests from parents of young or intermediate-level athletes for copies of training programs used by university-level athletes. If developed correctly, programs from one level of athletic ability don't transfer to other levels. Each group requires different volume, intensity, and load assignments for training to be effective. Young, inexperienced athletes are no match for an advanced-level program. Safety has to come first. Three training age groups are addressed in this chapter: a beginner group with no or little training experience, an intermediate group with a medium amount of training experience, and an advanced group with a lot of training experience. The training time allocations are suggestions and may have to be adjusted as mentioned before if you have competition conflicts. We provide a table that summarizes the yearly phases, themes, and training focus, as well as specific programs for each phase.

Beginner Group—No to Little Training Experience

The main goal with this group (8 to 13 years old) is to build a training foundation. This group includes young athletes beginning organized training for the first time as well as those with limited time. The overall plan should consist of mostly preparation work to learn techniques and acquire the foundational skills necessary to elevate training to the next stage. The time spent in competition mode should be about 15 percent of the total activity time. There also should be some attention to recovery and regeneration for players at this level, especially if they have multiple seasons. Cross-training with other activities and setting aside time just to be kids will help balance their overall development.

Speed

Speed development in this group should consist of learning basic running mechanics and working on tempo and coordination. Acceleration can be used in all speed workouts and can involve using small hills, ramps, or stairs.

Focus Exercises

Stationary leg drive drill for acceleration posture and leg drive, 4 × 10 seconds with 30-second rests between sets.

Walking Mach A drill, 2 × 30 yards, and walking Mach B drill, 2 × 30 yards.

Starts from various positions (staggered, lateral, diagonal step, and drop step) for 15 yards. Do 3 repetitions of each position and walk back to the starting point for recovery.

Get-ups, 2 sets of 5 repetitions for 20 yards, walk back for recovery.

All of these exercises can be performed twice a week.

Agility and Balance

Knowledge of stopping mechanics, lowering the center of gravity, and proper footwork mechanics will set a foundation for more intense change-of-direction drills. Balance training will teach you how to lower your center of gravity while in motion. Develop footwork through line drills and rope jumping.

Focus Exercises

Single-leg squat and reach out, 1 × 10 each leg, holding bottom squat position for 3 seconds.

Oregon shift drill, 2 × 5 each leg with no step and work up to 2 × 5 with one or two steps.

Line footwork drills, 2 × each drill for 10 seconds (forward/backward shuffling, alternating single step, alternating crossover step).

Rope jumping, 4-5 × 25 using single-foot and two-foot hopping side to side.

Wheel drill × 2 using one- and three-step progression.

Execute these drills twice a week.

Strength and Power

Develop body-weight exercises before adding resistance while using multijoint exercises (squat and press, lunge and reach) that challenge strength, coordination, and balance. The volume of training should be high to increase work capacity and capabilities for future training.

Strength Focus Exercises

Total-body strength training circuit. Use the following exercises in a circuit fashion with the protocol of 2 or 3 sets, 10 to 15 repetitions, and 30- to 60-second rests between sets: Standing band press (light tension band), upper-body step-up (forward and lateral), body row, physioball leg curl, standing medicine ball twist, and body bridge (15 to 20 sec. hold).

In addition, perform the basic half leg circuit (squat × 10, lunge × 5, step-up [12 to 18 in., or 30 to 45 cm, box] × 5 each leg, and squat jump × 5) using body weight for resistance. Do 2 or 3 sets and work up to 5 sets with 30- to 45-second rests between sets. As you progress, you can increase to 3 or 4 full leg circuit sets with 1-minute rests between sets. Perform the strength circuit twice a week during the off-season and once a week during the competitive phase.

Power Focus Exercises

Landing mechanics: Two-foot and single-leg stability jumps and hops, 2 × 5-10 with a 3-second hold.

Minihurdle multidirectional hops: Use five 6-inch (15 cm) hurdles and perform double-leg and single-leg hops, 2 × 5 of each variation.

Lateral bounds (ice skaters): Perform 2-3 × 10 (5 × each leg).

Use power drills once a week during the off-season and reduce the volume (reps and sets) by half during competition periods.

Conditioning

Anaerobic and aerobic pathways should be stimulated while developing work capacity through volume-based training.

Conditioning Focus

Conditioning for the beginner group is addressed through the volume of the preceding strength, power, agility, and balance exercises while keeping rest intervals minimal. This is in addition to practice sessions in which small-sided playing helps conditioning. Speed endurance can be trained using sprint repeats from 5 to 15 repetitions at various distances (20 to 60 yd.) and a limited rest period between (20 to 30 sec.). Perform up to twice a week at the end of workouts that aren't strenuous.

Beginner Group—No to Low Training Experience (Single Competition Period)

Month	Phase	Theme	Component emphasis
January February	Preparation	Learn how to train Strong and healthy	High volume General strength Balance training
March April May	Competition I Competition II	Speed and strength Speed and strength Strong and fit	Acceleration and general strength Anaerobic fitness
June July	Transition Active rest	Recovery from season	Cross-training activities
August	Active rest		
September	Preparation I	Regain strength and speed	General strength and acceleration/agility
October November	Preparation II Noncompetition	Soccer strong and fit	Special strength Speed endurance
December	Transition	Active rest	Cross-training activities

Intermediate Group—Medium Amount of Training Experience

Athletes in this group (14 to 17 years old) are in puberty (some junior high and early high school players). The objective for this group is to continue developing foundational fitness components with a shift toward more competition. Preparation work is still a priority, but it is more specific, and the competition time is doubled usually because of a second competition period with soccer club teams. Typically, female players' skills tend to be more advanced than males' at this point. Also, with the additional competition time, recovery time needs to increase to match the extra workload.

Speed

This should be a continuation of developing acceleration skills using hills, ramps, or light resistance (vest, sand, resistance cord). Increase reactive strength by using low-level plyometrics (hops and jumps).

Focus Exercises

Stationary leg drive drill, 3 sets × 10 seconds.

Acceleration starts: Get-ups, 2 × 5 repetitions, and get up and chase drill with a partner × 6 repetitions with walk-back recovery.

Three variations from hop or jump and go series of starts and acceleration, 1 set of each × 5 repetitions.

Short hill sprints: Use a slight grade hill or ramp for 30 yards and perform 5 sprints with a walk-back recovery.

Sprint in, sprint out: Use 60 yards with the second third (20 yd.) as the sprint zone. Perform 5 repetitions.

Execute drills once a week during noncompetitive phases and the first, second, and fifth drills during competition periods.

Agility and Balance

Intensity level can increase through programmed drills that involve cutting and changes of direction. Begin using reactive movement drills, some with a ball. Use footwork drills for dynamic balance.

Balance Focus Exercises

Single-leg squat, 2 × 3 each leg and hold bottom position for 10 seconds.

Dynamic balance hop: Use foam pad or perform barefooted on grass.

Single-leg hop and hold, landing for 3 seconds. Perform 3 sets of 3 repetitions on each leg (forward, backward, and sideways).

Agility Focus Exercises

Line footwork drill, 2 sets of each variation (shuffle, crossover, and single step forward and backward) × 10 each.

ABC ladder drill: Use single step forward, double step forward, double step lateral, diagonal shuffle step forward, and crossover step forward and backward. Perform two full lengths of each as fast as you can control.

Outside cutting drill: Use six cones in a zigzag pattern 6 yards apart, 2 × 5 repetitions with 2-minute rest between sets.

Cone drill: Use basic movements (sprint, shuffle, backpedal) and perform 2 repetitions starting from each side with 25-second rest between sets.

Strength and Power

Continue increasing general strength with an emphasis on increasing power. Functional core strength with rotational involvement will improve speed and explosiveness on the field. Pay attention to rest periods because of increased work intensity.

Strength Focus Exercises

Dumbbell squats, lunges, and step-ups, dumbbell single-leg squats, dumbbell squat jumps, body-weight full leg circuits.

Dumbbell bench chest press, push-up series (incline and decline position), body row, dumbbell shoulder complex. For weighted exercises, perform 3 sets for 6 to 8 repetitions.

Full leg circuits involve squat × 20, lunge × 20, step-up × 20, and squat jump × 10. Do 2 to 4 sets.

Core exercises: Back extension, medicine ball seated rotation, vertical chop, diagonal chop, body bridge. Perform 2 or 3 sets of 10 to 12 repetitions.

Strength train two or three times a week during noncompetition phases and once or twice a week during in-season periods. If you are training only 1 day a week during the season, make that day a total-body workout (lower, upper, and core).

Power Focus Exercises

Single-leg stability hops, 2 × 5 each leg.

Wheel drill, 2 or 3 sets × 1 and 3 steps.

Multidirectional hurdle jumps, 2 or 3 sets × 5 jumps (18 in., or 45 cm, hurdle).

Low box jumps: Use 18- to 21-inch (45 to 53 cm) boxes. Perform 2 or 3 sets of 5 repetitions. Land softly and step back down to reset.

Lateral bounds (ice skaters), 2 or 3 sets of 20 repetitions.

Power train twice a week during noncompetitive phases and once a week during the in-season with the total volume cut in half.

Conditioning

Peak conditioning levels at precompetition phases to increase readiness for the season. Emphasis can begin to shift to more intensity and less volume. Focus on speed endurance using various workloads to vary the intensity (distances and intensities).

Conditioning Focus Workouts

300-yard shuttles: Use a 25- or 50-yard distance and perform 2 to 4 repetitions with a 3:1 rest-to-work interval.

Sprint-jog-walk: Sprint 10 seconds, jog 20 seconds, and walk 10 seconds for 5- to 10-minute segments. Rest 2 minutes and repeat twice.

Dribble and shoot: Perform 2 sets of 4 repetitions and rest 90 seconds between repetitions.

Fartlek training: Perform 2 or 3 repetitions of 3 to 5 minutes using a 30-second run, 30-second jog continuous tempo. Walk 2 minutes between segments.

Perform conditioning work no more than twice a week outside of the competition phase and once a week during heavy competition phases.

Intermediate Group—Medium Amount of Training Experience (Double Competition)

Month	Phase	Theme	Component emphasis
January	Preparation I	Strong and fast	Build strength Develop acceleration and speed technique
February	Preparation II	Get ready to compete Fitness peak	Special strength Anaerobic conditioning
March April	Competition I Competition II	Strong, fast, and healthy	Strength endurance Acceleration and speed endurance Injury prevention
May	Championship season Transition	Win the match and recover Active rest	Strength and recovery Cross-training
June July	Preparation I Preparation II	Get working again! Strong and fast	Increase work capacity Build back strength, work acceleration, and speed
August September October	Precompetition Competition I Competition II	Power and fitness Stay strong and healthy Stay fit and strong	Reactive strength Anaerobic conditioning Strength endurance and lower-body injury prevention
November December	Championship season Transition Noncompetition	Win and recover Active recovery Get working again!	Strength and recovery Cross-training

Advanced Group—A Lot of Training Experience

The final group includes athletes in postpuberty (18 years and older). Physical training emphasis now becomes training to win the match. Some of the players in this group will have double competition periods during the year as well as be playing at a higher level of competition. There will be less emphasis on preparation work because more time is devoted to competition, which will warrant a second recovery (transition) period. Athletes in this group are also more apt to attempt to peak the training during certain points throughout the training year because of their advanced experience and mastery of the previous two stages (beginner and intermediate levels).

Speed

Fine-tuning speed mechanics and the use of advanced speed techniques (resisted and top-end speed drills) can be introduced at this stage. Soccer-specific acceleration drills (with a ball) using multiple directions will become the emphasis. Advanced plyometric drills (double- and single-leg bounds) can be incorporated.

Focus Drills

Walking Mach A drill, 2×20 yards, skipping Mach A drill, 2×20 yards

Get up and chase drill, 2×5, with a partner or rolled soccer ball, walk-back recovery.

180-degree turn and go, $3 \times$ right turn, $3 \times$ left turn, and accelerate for 20 yards, walk-back recovery.

Single-leg hop and go, 2 sets $\times$ 4 repetitions each leg, accelerate 20 yards, walk-back recovery.

Medicine ball over the back and go: Use a 3-kilogram (6.6 lb.) medicine ball. Perform 2 or 3 sets of 4 repetitions. Sprint 20 yards. Walk back to recover.

Sled towing or hill sprints: Perform 5 to 10 repetitions for hill sprints of 20 to 40 yards. Walk down the hill for recovery. Do 4 to 6 repetitions for sled towing of 30 to 60 yards. Use between 10 and 25 percent of your body weight as resistance on the sled (e.g., a 150 lb. [68 kg] athlete would use between 15 and 40 lb. [6.8-18 kg]).

S-curve runs and sprint in, sprint out: Use these drills for top-end speed work. Perform curve runs with a partner for distances from 25 to 60 meters. Do 2 sets of 4 repetitions with 90-second rests between reps and 3 minutes between sets.

In and outs: Perform 4 to 6 repetitions with a 3:1 rest-to-work ratio.

Perform speed drills twice a week, choosing three drills for each workout during off-season training periods. Use only acceleration drills during the in-season to maintain match sharpness.

Agility and Balance

Balance, footwork, and agility training are more reactive to simulate match-like decisions that will help performance on the field.

Agility Focus Drills

ABC ladder drills: Perform footwork drills using forward, backward, lateral, and crossover maneuvers along with two-foot and one-foot hopping through the ladder. Do 2 repetitions of each drill. Progress to using half ladders that are 5 yards apart. Perform the footwork through each ladder, accelerating between and out of the ladders.

Minihurdles, forward and backward shuffling: Do 4 to 6 sets with 20-second recoveries between sets.

Hurdler sampler: Perform 3 sets with 20-second recoveries between them.

Outside-inside cut drill: Zigzag pattern for 20 yards. Perform 3 sets for the outside cut and 3 sets for the inside cut. Recover 30 seconds between sets.

Compass drill: Perform 2 repetitions starting right and 2 starting left. Rest 30 seconds between sets.

Pro agility shuttle: Do 3 sets of 3 repetitions with 20 seconds of rest between repetitions and 1 minute between sets.

Reactive position drills: Using your position-specific drill, perform 3 to 5 sets with the prescribed rest periods.

Perform agility work twice a week during the off-season and once a week with half the volume during competitive phases.

Balance Focus Drills

Single-leg squat (barefooted), 1 × 8 each leg (eyes open), 1 × 8 each leg (one eye closed).

Single-leg squat with ball toss: Partner tosses ball to pass back and forth, 1 × 8 each leg.

Minihurdle lateral hop to single-leg landing: Perform 4 sets of 2 repetitions starting each way (right or left). Recover 20 seconds between repetitions.

Lateral bound with landing: Perform 2 sets forward and backward, holding the landing for 2 seconds. Recover 1 minute between sets.

Single-leg squat drills can be performed daily as part of a workout warm-up. Hurdles and jumping and bounding are performed once or twice a week in the off-season and once with half the volume during the season.

Strength and Power

Introduce more traditional exercises (front/back squat, power clean) for resistance training. Increase dynamic core strength and mobility through resistance cords, cables, or medicine balls. Increase the intensity of injury prevention exercises.

Strength Focus Exercises

Barbell back squat, dumbbell lunge, step-up, dumbbell split squat, single-leg Romanian deadlift, physioball leg curl, barbell and dumbbell chest press, rotational shoulder press, seated pull-down, dumbbell row: Perform 2 to 4 sets and 8 to 12 repetitions with an intensity of 70 to 85 percent of 1RM.

Core strength: Back extensions, bench rotating sit-ups, hanging knee raises, medicine ball vertical chops, medicine ball single-leg figure eights; 2 sets and 12 to 15 repetitions.

During off-season training, perform strength exercises two or three times a week. Rotate two or three exercises per area (upper body, lower body, core) for each workout. During the season, cut the total volume in half and lower the intensity (60 to 75 percent of 1RM).

Power Focus Exercises

Medicine ball total-body throws: Use squat and push, squat and scoop, and over the back; 2 sets of 3 to 5 repetitions. Rest 45 seconds between sets. Use a 3- to 5-kilogram (6.6-11 lb.) medicine ball.

Box jumps: Use boxes from knee height to waist height to increase intensity. Perform 2 or 3 sets of 5 or 6 repetitions.

Bounding: Use double-leg forward bounds, lateral bounds (ice skaters), and single-leg forward bounds; 2 or 3 sets of 5 to 10 repetitions. Rest 2 minutes between sets.

Perform one or two power drills twice a week during training cycles and once a week with half the volume during competition phases.

Conditioning

Training volume can reflect speed endurance with increased intensity. Interval runs and shuttle runs can be the main method of conditioning.

Conditioning Focus Workouts

120s: Begin with 6 repetitions with the prescribed work and rest times. Increase 1 repetition every 2 weeks until you reach 10.

Small-sided games (1v1): Perform 4 sets with 90 seconds of recovery between sets.

Position pattern runs: Perform 2 or 3 sets with 5-minute breaks between sets.

One-minute sprint shuttles, 300-yard shuttles: Perform 3 to 5 sets with a 3:1 rest-to-work ratio.

Use conditioning runs twice a week in the off-season and once a week during the season.

Advanced Group—A Lot of Training Experience (One Major Competitive Season)

Month	Phase	Theme	Component emphasis
January February	Noncompetition I Noncompetition II	Build work capacity Get stronger and faster	Teaching techniques—acceleration drills and basic strength
March April	Training with light competition Testing/evaluation	Train and play Did the training work?	Reactive strength and speed development Athletic test battery
May	Transition	Recover and regenerate	Physical and mental recovery
June July	Preparation I Preparation II	Get strong and fast Peak performance	Strength, speed, and agility work Power training Anaerobic conditioning
August	Precompetition	Get ready to compete	Strength endurance
September October	Competition I Competition II	Stay strong, fast, and healthy	Strength endurance Injury prevention Speed endurance
November December	Championship season Transition	Every match is important Get rested	Peak power and recovery Active rest

SAMPLE TRAINING PROGRAMS

This section offers a yearly training cycle (preparation, precompetition, competition, and transition periods) showing sample workout plans by training group (beginner, intermediate, and advanced).

Noncompetition: General Preparation Phase
Theme: Building Work Capacity

Training group	Beginner	Intermediate	Advanced
Flexibility	Dynamic flexibility with crawling (shuffle, carioca, Spiderman), 2 sets of 10 steps right and left	Dynamic flexibility Hurdle step-overs (forward-backward-side), 2 × 5 Low, slow carioca	Dynamic flexibility Hurdle under and over (forward-backward-side), 2 × 5 Oregon shift drill, 3 × 5 each leg
Balance	Single-leg squat and hold (5 sec.), 2 sets each leg Medicine ball overhead squat, 2 × 10	Lunge and reach, three-way, 1 × 3 each leg Lunge and twist, three-way, 1 × 3 each leg Lunge with overhead reach, three-way, 1 × 3 each leg	Overhead squat, 2 × 10 Single-leg hop and hold (3 sec.), forward-side-rotational, 1 × 3 each leg
Speed and agility	Speed ladder basic, 2 × 6 drills Seated arm swings, 3 × 15 sec. Wall drill, 3 × 10 sec. Falling starts × 5	Speed ladder basic, 2 × 6 drills Falling starts × 5 Partner resistance starts × 5 Get-up starts × 5	Speed ladder with starts × 6 drills Jump/hop restarts × 5 Get-up starts × 5 Short stair sprints, 20 steps × 5
Strength and power	Circuit train: Incline pull-ups, incline push-ups, 2 × 10-12 reps each Half leg circuit (body weight): squat, lunge, step-up, squat jump, 3 sets, 30 sec. rest	Circuit train: Incline pull-ups, incline push-ups, dumbbell multidirectional lunge and reach, squat jumps, 3 × 10 reps each exercise with 1 min. rests between sets	Circuit train: Pull-ups, band standing press, dumbbell curl and press, 3 × 10 each or 30 sec. interval Full leg circuit (vest): squat, lunge, step-up, squat jump × 3 sets with 1 min. rests between
Core training	Multiple plank holds, front and back, 15 sec. each × 2 sets Medicine ball standing rotations (twist-chop series) × 5 each way	Medicine ball standing rotations (twist-chop series) × 8 each way Superman raise, 2 × 12 Rotational crunch, 2 × 15	Medicine ball rotations (twist-chop series) × 10 each way Back extension, 2 × 15 Three-position crunch, 2 × 20
Conditioning	Continuous jump rope, two-foot hops, 5 × 1 min.	8 × 2 min. run @75% 1 min. fast walk between sets	6 min. run test Use score for future conditioning
Cool-down	Static stretch	Static stretch	Static stretch

Precompetition: Power and Conditioning Phase
Theme: Practice and Match Readiness

Training group	Beginner	Intermediate	Advanced
Flexibility	Dynamic flexibility Oregon shift drill, 3 × 10	Dynamic flexibility Hurdle step-overs (forward-backward-side), × 5 each Low, slow carioca, 2 × 10 steps	Dynamic flexibility Hurdle under and overs (forward-backward-side), × 5 each Oregon shift drill, 3 × 10
Balance	Single-leg squat, 2 × 5 each Single-leg hop and hold (front-side-rotate), 3 sec. hold, 1 × 3 each way	Single-leg squat, 2 × 5 each Single-leg hurdle (6 in., or 15 cm) Hops, front-side, 2 × 5 each way	Medicine ball single-leg squat and reach, 1 × 10 each leg BOSU two-foot hop to hold, 3 sec., 2 × 5
Speed and agility	Half-speed ladder to multidirectional acceleration, 2 × forward, 2 × backward, 2 × each side	Soccer-specific starts (from jog, backpedal, shuffle, jump, or pass), 2 × each way	Soccer-specific starts (with ball), × 6
Strength and power	Pull-up, push-up, squat, multidirectional lunge, squat jump, lateral bound (ice skater), body weight, 2 × 10 each exercise	Pull-up, push-up, squat, multidirectional lunge, step-up, dip, squat jump, lateral bound (ice skater) with vest, dumbbells, 3 × 8 each exercise	Pull-up, dumbbell bench press, row, curl and press, lunge, squat, multidirectional jump, 3 × 8 each exercise
Core training	Medicine ball total-body throws (pushing, chopping, rotating), × 2 each throw	Medicine ball wall throws (squat and push, side rotational, squat and scoop, over the back), × 5 each	Medicine ball wall throws, × 10 each
Conditioning	Speed endurance (20-50 yd.), 5 × 20 yd., 2 × 30 yd., 2 × 40 yd., 1 × 50 yd.	Speed endurance (20-80 yd.), 5 × 20 yd., 2 × 40 yd., 2 × 50 yd., 1 × 80 yd.	Speed endurance (60-120 yd.), 2 × 60 yd. (75%), 5 × 120 yd.
Cool-down	Static stretch	Static stretch	Static stretch

Competition: Maintenance Phase
Theme: Strong, Fit, and Healthy

Training group	Beginner	Intermediate	Advanced
Flexibility	Practice warm-up: Dynamic flexibility, 10-12 min.	Dynamic flexibility Hurdle step-overs (forward-backward-side), × 5 each way Low, slow carioca, 2 × 10 steps	Dynamic flexibility Hurdle under and over (forward-backward-side), × 4 sets Oregon shift drill, 2 × 10
Balance	Minihurdle hops, 2 × 5 each leg (double leg, single leg)	Minihurdle hops, 2 × 5 each leg (single-leg forward, side)	Single-leg squat and touch, 2 × 10 each leg
Speed and agility	Acceleration starts with ball, 2 × 5	Speed ladder with acceleration, × 6	Speed ladder with acceleration, × 6-8
Strength and power	On-field training: Body-weight squat, lunge, step-up with upper-body combination (reach, press, or rotate) with medicine ball × 20 sec. each exercise	Day 1: Weight vest/dumbbells, lower-body emphasis, squat, lunge, step-up, hamstring maintenance, 2 × 10 each exercise Day 2: Upper-body emphasis, core, and power training (medicine ball), 2 × 10 for exercises, × 5 for throws	Day 1: Lower-body emphasis, squat, lunge, step-up, hamstring maintenance, 2 × 10 reps Day 2: Upper-body emphasis, core, and power training (dumbbells and medicine balls), 2 × 10 for exercises, 3 × 5 for power exercises
Core training	Ab work with flexion, extension, and rotation, 5 × 12-15	Medicine ball wall throws (push, rotate, throw), 2 × 10 each	Total-body medicine ball throws (over, under, rotation), 2 × 10 each
Conditioning	Soccer practice and short-sided games (20-40 yd.), 5 × 20 yd., 5 × 40 yd.	Soccer practice drills and repeat sprints (30-50 yd.), 3 × 30 yd., 7 × 50 yd.	Soccer practice drills and repeat sprints (60-120 yd.), 2 × 5 × 60 yd.
Cool-down	Static stretch	Static stretch	Static stretch

Transition: Active Recovery Phase
Theme: Recover From Season and Regenerate

Training group	Beginner	Intermediate	Advanced
Flexibility	Dynamic flexibility, 20 min.	Dynamic flexibility or yoga, 30 min.	Dynamic flexibility or yoga, 30 min.
Balance	Flexibility workout	Yoga	Yoga
Speed and agility	Any cross-training activity: racquet sports, team sports (no soccer)	Any cross-training activity: racquet sports, team sports (no soccer)	Any cross-training activity: racquet sports, team sports (no soccer)
Strength and power	Body weight: calisthenics, body row, push-up series, lunge and squat	Body weight, strength endurance, body row, push-up series, lunge, squat, step-up	Body weight or light weight with high volume, all exercises 30 sec. interval
Core training	Body weight: flexion, extension, rotation, 2 × 15 of each	Light medicine ball standing rotations, 2 × 10	Light medicine ball standing rotations, 2 × 10
Conditioning	Cross-training: swim, bike, ease into some running, 20-30 min.	Cross-training: swim, bike, light running, 20-30 min.	Cross-training: swim, bike, light running, 30-45 min.
Cool-down	Static stretch	Static stretch	Static stretch

Given the incredible amount of information modern technology has put at our fingertips, constructing a total training program can be confusing as well as overwhelming. Balancing and adjusting the fitness components to meet your individual needs and achieve maximal results requires a conscious effort. Having explored the information in the previous chapters, you should now understand that conditioning training for soccer should be a vital part of every player's overall development. Neglecting certain components can hinder your progress toward becoming a top-level athlete, whereas overdoing training and concentrating too much on certain components can lead to imbalances in performance. This book prescribes an appropriate amount of training for your level of play. As you gain training experience, you will learn how your body becomes faster, quicker, and more powerful when playing in a match. Use *Complete Conditioning for Soccer* as your complete reference for training ideas to keep you playing at a high level for many years to come. Remember that soccer is still a game that brings out the basic athletic qualities of sport. Enjoy displaying these qualities on the pitch as you help your team reach its potential. Good luck on your training road to success!

Estimating 1RM From a Training Load

% of 1RM	100	93.5	91	88.5	86	83.5	81	78.5	76	73.5
Maximum repetitions	1	2	3	4	5	6	7	8	9	10
Weight lifted	5	5	5	4	4	4	4	4	4	4
	10	9	9	9	9	8	8	8	8	7
	15	14	14	13	13	13	12	12	11	11
	20	19	18	18	17	17	16	16	15	15
	25	23	23	22	22	21	20	20	19	18
	30	28	27	27	26	25	24	24	23	22
	35	33	32	31	30	29	28	28	27	26
	40	37	36	35	34	33	32	31	30	29
	45	42	41	40	39	38	37	35	34	33
	50	47	46	44	43	42	41	39	38	37
	55	51	50	49	47	46	45	43	42	40
	60	56	55	53	52	50	49	47	46	44
	65	61	59	58	56	54	53	51	49	48
	70	66	64	62	60	59	57	55	53	52
	75	70	68	66	65	63	61	59	57	55
	80	75	73	71	69	67	65	63	61	59
	85	80	77	75	73	71	69	67	65	63
	90	84	82	80	77	75	73	71	68	66
	95	89	87	84	82	79	77	75	72	70
	100	94	91	89	86	84	81	79	76	74
	105	98	96	93	90	88	85	82	80	77
	110	103	100	97	95	92	89	86	84	81
	115	108	105	102	99	96	93	90	87	85

(continued)

% of 1RM	100	93.5	91	88.5	86	83.5	81	78.5	76	73.5
Maximum repetitions	1	2	3	4	5	6	7	8	9	10
Weight lifted (continued)	120	112	109	106	103	100	97	94	91	88
	125	117	114	111	108	104	101	98	95	92
	130	122	118	115	112	109	105	102	99	96
	135	126	123	120	116	113	109	106	103	99
	140	131	127	124	120	117	113	110	106	103
	145	136	132	128	125	121	118	114	110	107
	150	140	137	133	129	125	122	118	114	110
	155	145	141	137	133	129	126	122	118	114
	160	150	146	142	138	134	130	126	122	118
	165	154	150	146	142	138	134	130	125	121
	170	159	155	151	146	142	138	134	129	125
	175	164	159	155	151	146	142	137	133	129
	180	168	164	159	155	150	146	141	137	132
	185	173	168	164	159	155	150	145	141	136
	190	178	173	168	163	159	154	149	144	140
	195	182	178	173	168	163	158	153	148	143
	200	187	182	177	172	167	162	157	152	147
	205	192	187	181	176	171	166	161	156	151
	210	196	191	186	181	175	170	165	160	154
	215	201	196	190	185	180	174	169	163	158
	220	206	200	195	189	184	178	173	167	162
	225	210	205	199	194	188	182	177	171	165
	230	215	209	204	198	192	186	181	175	169
	235	220	214	208	202	196	190	185	179	173
	240	224	218	212	206	200	194	188	182	176
	245	229	223	217	211	205	199	192	186	180
	250	234	228	221	215	209	203	196	190	184
	255	238	232	226	219	213	207	200	194	187
	260	243	237	230	224	217	211	204	198	191
	265	248	241	235	228	221	215	208	201	195
	270	253	246	239	232	226	219	212	205	199
	275	257	250	243	237	230	223	216	209	202

% of 1RM	100	93.5	91	88.5	86	83.5	81	78.5	76	73.5
Maximum repetitions	1	2	3	4	5	6	7	8	9	10
Weight lifted (continued)	280	262	255	248	241	234	227	220	213	206
	285	267	259	252	245	238	231	224	217	210
	290	271	264	257	249	243	235	228	220	213
	295	276	269	261	254	246	239	232	224	217
	300	281	273	266	258	251	243	236	228	221
	305	285	278	270	262	255	247	239	232	224
	310	290	282	274	267	259	251	243	236	228
	315	295	287	279	271	263	255	247	239	232
	320	299	291	283	275	267	259	251	243	235
	325	304	296	288	280	271	263	255	247	239
	330	309	300	292	284	276	267	259	251	243
	335	313	305	297	288	280	271	263	255	246
	340	318	309	301	292	284	275	267	258	250
	345	323	314	305	297	288	280	271	262	254
	350	327	319	310	301	292	284	275	266	257
	355	332	323	314	305	296	288	279	270	261
	360	337	328	319	310	301	292	283	274	265
	365	341	332	323	314	305	296	287	277	268
	370	346	337	328	318	309	300	291	281	272
	375	351	341	332	323	313	304	294	285	276
	380	355	346	336	327	317	308	298	289	279
	385	360	350	341	331	322	312	302	293	283
	390	365	355	345	335	326	316	306	296	287
	395	369	360	350	340	330	320	310	300	290
	400	374	364	354	344	334	324	314	304	294
	405	379	369	358	348	338	328	318	308	298
	410	383	373	363	353	342	332	322	312	301
	415	388	378	367	357	347	336	326	315	305
	420	393	382	372	361	351	340	330	319	309
	425	397	387	376	366	355	344	334	323	312
	430	402	391	381	370	359	348	338	327	316
	435	407	396	385	374	363	352	342	331	320

(continued)

% of 1RM	100	93.5	91	88.5	86	83.5	81	78.5	76	73.5
Maximum repetitions	1	2	3	4	5	6	7	8	9	10
Weight lifted (continued)	440	411	400	389	378	367	356	345	334	323
	445	416	405	394	383	372	361	349	338	327
	450	421	410	398	387	376	365	353	342	331
	455	425	414	403	391	380	369	357	346	334

Bibliography

Bompa, T.O. 1994. *Theory and methodology of training: The key to athletic performance.* 3rd ed. Dubuque, IA: Kendall/Hunt.

Clark, M.A., and A.M. Russell. 2001. *NASM-OPT course manual: Optimum performance training for the performance enhancement specialist.* 1st ed. Calabasas, CA: National Academy of Sports Medicine.

Gambetta, V. 2007. *Athletic development.* Champaign, IL: Human Kinetics.

National Strength and Conditioning Association. 1994. *Essentials of strength training and conditioning.* Edited by T.R. Baechle. Champaign, IL: Human Kinetics.

Pearson, A. 2001. *SAQ soccer.* London: A&C Black.

Radcliffe, J.C., and R.C. Farentinos. 1999. *High-powered plyometrics.* Champaign, IL: Human Kinetics.

Radcliffe, J.C. 2007. *Functional training for athletes at all levels.* Berkeley, CA: Ulysses Press.

Index

Note: The italicized *f* and *t* following page numbers refer to figures and tables, respectively.